A Guide To Passionate, Purposeful Blogging

By Demetria Zinga

Copyright © 2016 by Demetria Zinga
All rights reserved.

This book is licensed for your personal enjoyment only. This ebook may not be re-sold or given away to other people. If you would like to share this book with another person, please purchase an additional copy for each recipient. This book or any portion thereof may not be reproduced or used in any manner whatsoever without the express written permission of the publisher except for the use of brief quotations in a book review. Thank you for respecting the hard work of this author.

For questions and more information, please contact:

Mompreneurs In Heels
PO Box 15
Palo Alto, CA 94304

http://www.mompreneursinheels.com/

TABLE OF CONTENTS

DEDICATION

INTRODUCTION

CHAPTER 1: "WHY MOMPRENEURS?"

CHAPTER 2: DISCOVER YOUR PASSIONS

CHAPTER 3: OVERCOMING BUSINESS FEARS

CHAPTER 4: RESEARCH

CHAPTER 5: SET UP A BEAUTIFULLY SUCCESSFUL BLOG

CHAPTER 6: POSITION YOURSELF AS AN EXPERT

CHAPTER 7: DEVELOP THE PERFECT BLOGGING ROUTINE

CHAPTER 8: MAKE FABULOUS, LIKE-MINDED CONNECTIONS

CHAPTER 9: FIND YOUR STRIDE AND WORK IT!

CHAPTER 10: TIME TO CELEBRATE!

DEDICATION

This book was written completely on faith and a whim, along with some coffee and all-nighters! Without the support of family and friends, I wouldn't have been able to move forward on this project.

So, I want to thank you.

First of all- to my God, my Best Friend, Guide, & Mentor- Jesus. You are the reason I am privileged to be a mompreneur. I'm thankful you're my CEO!

To my dear husband, Bob Fabien- I am so honored to be your wife. Your support has been a-MA-zing! Thanks for always pushing me to keep going even when I wanted to give up. Double thanks for hanging out with the kids while I ran to the local cafe to finish writing, and for helping me through decisions on publishing, formatting, and marketing. You were also my trusty editor. I love you SO much, and I could not have done this without you!

To my wonderful kids- thank you for being so super supportive of your mommy these past months as I've written, written, and rewritten. My beautiful teen daughter, Nyomi- your help means so much to me. Thanks for taking up my slack, helping around the house, and entertaining your little sister for me while I work. You are such a gem! To my sweet little girl, Zoe- you have such an understanding heart. I appreciate all the times you've stayed busy while I work in the office. I love being your mommy!

To my parents, thank you for just being there even though we're far away. Just knowing you have my best interest at heart is enough for me. You've always been huge supporters and ongoing cheerleaders for me. I love you always.

To my designers and reviewers, and everyone else who has played a part in seeing this book come to fruition-thank you so much.

And to all of my subscribers, viewers, listeners, and followers at Web Success Coaching and Mompreneurs In Heels- a HUGE thank you! You are my main inspiration for this book and the reason I do what I do.

Introduction

As a mompreneur, I know what it's like to have a dream to start your own business, although you may feel completely overwhelmed with the idea of it.

Over a decade ago, I found out some things about myself. I learned that I had untapped desires for business ideas and that anything was possible.

I had just given birth to our first daughter, and my husband was finishing up graduate school while I worked a full-time job at our local university. Neither he nor I saw it coming, but a passion for business began brewing in my heart and I soon became obsessed with the idea of starting up my side hustle so that I could leave my 9-5.

Within two years of my daughter being born, I had started up two businesses: one sweet handmade soaps biz and another developing passion: in website design. Both of these business projects taught me much of what I know today about the ins and outs of setting up shop online. I've made plenty of mistakes along the way, and I've also made some pretty decent decisions.

One of the best decisions I've made was to begin blogging- (back in 2006 when it was a newer concept), and helping other women in business to do the same. I've seen the amazing outcomes of women who have taken their online businesses to the next level with a simple blog. I've watched women with purpose begin to formulate those passions into credible business ideas, and create an online business presence that attracts the masses.

I teach women entrepreneurs and mom bloggers how to

start and maintain an online business through passionate, purposeful blogging- and I love what I do. I believe this book is an essential ingredient to your success as an online business owner.

If you've been sitting on the edge of your seat, waiting for your money-making opportunity to happen, then this book will give you a jump start in the right direction. In fact, you'll be jostled from sitting on your seat into taking action and laying a foundation for your future blogging success.

In this book, I'll teach you how to **recognize** your gifts, talents, and passion, **determine** your business purpose and **create** a business vision. With these three essential ingredients, you'll be paving the way to business profits.

Along the way we'll also uncover ways to make your voice unique to your business, as well as locate the best target market for you, create a customer avatar, and establish an easy-peasy blogging routine that keeps your products at the forefront of your prospects' minds!

Whether you're a newbie blogger converting your current business establishment to an online venue or turning your hobby blog into a virtual business establishment, this book will help you, and I'm here to help you each step of the way.

Ready to get started? Let's go!

Chapter 1: Why "Mompreneurs"?

What's Your Scenario?

Are you *that mom* who desires to start her own business? I mean, it's not that you don't like being on the PTA, or shuttling your kids to soccer practice every Wednesday evening. But you've got this little, nagging desire deep down inside that just won't go away. Whether it's being 110% involved in your child's school, chauffeuring your kids around town to extracurricular activities, taking care of a newborn round the clock, chasing behind a toddler all day long, or even homeschooling your kids, you're knee-deep in the trenches of parenthood.

Perhaps you're a working mom who clocks in at the office every morning at a punctual 8:00 and doesn't have a second to herself past five because you have somewhere else you need to be. The kids are waiting for you to pick them up from school only to drive them to soccer, ballet, and piano lessons, and then you need to swing by the dry cleaners, pick up take-out for dinner on the way home, and throw in a load of laundry once you get home because you didn't have time to finish last week's dirty load. The kids are exhausted and so are you. Your husband comes home late from work again but still has a few phone meetings so as he tucks away in your home office you head off to bathe the little kids and help your older ones with homework. You need some sleep and so do the kids. It's late and everyone is cranky. It's at this point that you wonder why you'll be getting up at 6 a.m. the next morning just to start this routine all over again.

What if you could be in control of your time- in charge of your own schedule? What if you had more flexibility to take care of your kids and family without the structure of your 8-5 job? You were just thinking that you have some hobbies that might be possible to turn into a business. Could you start your own business? Is it possible? Are you crazy for even thinking about the possibility?

Maybe you've been a stay at home mom for a few years now. Although the kids are growing older you still have some young ones in tow. You love being home with your kids and the flexibility being a stay at home mom provides you and your children...but for once you'd just like to feel someone tugging at you for something other than a sippy cup with juice. And you'd like to listen to your favorite radio station and work at your hobbies again rather than hear another few hours of Nick Jr. (though I love that channel, don't get me wrong!)

And just what if your hobbies could bring you some profit online? Could you build a business around your hobbies? Could you work a business around your baby's nap schedule?

Maybe you homeschool your kids and your days are swamped with responsibilities: cooking, cleaning, playdates, lessons, learning groups and coops, music lessons, church- not to mention time with each individual kid (outside of school work) and time with the husband. But you've always had a longing in the back of your heart and a fire burning deep inside.

Maybe you're an artist. Maybe you design and sew children's clothing. You thought about selling on Etsy and maybe creating a business blog to help you accomplish your goals faster. But with all the daily grind of responsibilities, how will you find the time?

These are just a few scenarios of which you might find yourself. If you can't find yourself in these examples, you have your own story and reasons you have come to the crossroads where you are today. If you aren't beginning a business but need to figure out how to take your current blogging platform to the next level, I hear ya. And I'm here to help.

Let's switch gears a bit as I bring some light to why entrepreneurial women are important to our society, and why I believe moms who have the passion for business should tread this path at least once - and hopefully to continue along the path as your life journey allows.

What do mompreneurs offer?

I totally get it. Sometimes it's hard to envision yourself working one second beyond what's required of you at home, let alone create a sustainable business you're passionate about.

If you have ever felt the need to express a side of you that goes beyond the existence of parenthood and taps into a part of your soul that brings you to life, brings the best out of you, allows you to soar, *and you get to make money while doing it,* then you've discovered the mompreneur inside, my friend!

Welcome to the club. Many moms like myself have been bitten by the mompreneur bug.

This book is all about giving you the permission or the motivation (whichever you need) to tap into your desires for entrepreneurship, reach deep inside to find out what you can offer the world, then equip you with step by step action guides to help you begin your business through the power of blogging. I also want to help you figure out a way to balance your business with your family. I don't want you burning the candle at both ends!

So, who are mompreneurs?

In today's world, the term "mom entrepreneur" is no longer an oxymoron. Come to think of it, I'm not sure that it ever truly was. Mom entrepreneurs (or "mompreneurs") go way back to bible days. No kidding. The woman referenced in Proverbs 31 is described as watching over the ways of her household while "considering fields" and buying them. This proverbial woman was into real estate, and with her profits, she was able to afford a wardrobe that might be greater than or equal in worth and sophistication to today's finest designer clothing. How's that for ancient success?

Think of all the big names and successful women who happen to also be doing one of the greatest works on earth: mothering. The two don't need to be mutually exclusive (motherhood and business). Women entrepreneurs in general have made a major impression on our society- so much so, that major brands develop product lines and make business decisions based on the buying and selling power of women. You see, they know we women rock and here's why:

- When we buy or sell, women are passionate.
- Women are motivated.
- Women know what we want.
- We know how to get what we want.
- We know how to influence our friends' purchasing decisions.

The influence of women in the marketplace is unquestionably real.

According to Punchbowl.com, one in every three bloggers

are moms and the average household income of a mom blogger is- get this- $84,000! While this figure, of course, is definitely not the baseline for the majority of mom bloggers, it pays to take a look at the potential of taking your online business blogging seriously. Additionally, mom bloggers have some real influential power since 55% of social media moms will make purchases based on recommendations from a blog review.

The reason these stats are important is because it gives you an idea of how influential you can be in your business- if you're passionate and purposeful.

However, motherhood beckons. Let's briefly address the complexities of being a mompreneur before we move on.

The perceived "setback"

Many moms all over the world have discovered after the birth of our children how much of our true selves get buried underneath the monotony of everyday life. After having children, we get caught up in the process of being a mom and wearing the mommy hat at all times. The mommy hat is a comfortable hat and we never take it off. From the time we bring our cute little babies home from the hospital for the very first time until the time they've graduated high school and begun a new life for themselves, we find ourselves constantly wearing the mommy hat.

Sometimes, instead of a hat, I like to use the analogy of **shoes.** Imagine with me, if you will:

You slip into your comfy, cozy slippers when you get out of the shower and pour yourself a cup of morning coffee or tea.

As your kids are piling out of the bed to start their school day, you kick off the slippers and lace up your sneakers. It's going to be a long day ahead- shuttling your kids back and forth from school activities.

Upon your arrival home, you open your closet to find those cute 3-inch heels you've been wanting to wear for years. The shoes are beckoning you, calling you- but to no avail. Those shoes represent the promotion you received years ago at the law firm you used to work for. Your powerful executive position- the one job you had that made you feel in charge. Maybe the heels represent your future career in advertising. Or maybe the heels represent an under-utilized gift or talent that has potential but needs to stay on the shelf for a while as you raise your kids.

If the shoes represent your past, you back away from the closet and close the door, with a bit of disappointment. Those shoes no longer seem to hold any relevance to you today. Today, you don't feel in charge- because who can control when the baby wakes up from his nap, or what the teacher will say about your kid during a tough school day?

Today? Today, your sneakers and slippers are your comfort zone.

But...if only.

The comeback.

Sometimes you stare longingly at those shiny heels and wish there was some way you could have the best of both worlds. To somehow be able to merge your work life with your home life and be able to do what you love as a professional, but still be completely available as a wife, a mom, and a friend would be the picture of perfection.

You think, "Isn't that too good to be true?"

Hear me out when I say that it's *not* impossible. You *can* have the best of both worlds. It's time to make a comeback, and with the support of your family and friends, get moving in the direction of figuring out how to have both your cake and your icing.

Don't ever let anyone tell you that it can't be done. I know too many successful moms out there who have done it, and are enjoying their slice of the pie. And yes, there's plenty of pie to go around. You can have your slice of it, too.

You see, your setback is not really a setback at all. The raising of your kids is actually the best investment you can make in not only your family but yourself because it causes you to reach way past your comfort zone and tap into unique gifts you never knew you had.

I found out over ten years ago when I resigned from my job in order to raise my daughter who was 15 months old at the time, that although I closed the door to one avenue of income, I opened my world to fresh opportunities and multiple streams of income. I began to soar like a free bird who had been caged up in her cubicle for far too long. I loved the freedom entrepreneurship gave me. From selling lotions and handmade soaps to designing websites, writing and selling e-courses, and earning website ad revenues, I had tapped into a new arena of "work", where the 9 to 5 timesheet was no longer my master.

The amazing thing is, I loved my new line of work, which didn't feel like work at all. And I absolutely loved having a home office right next to my baby's bedroom so that when she woke up from her nap I could step just a few feet away to pick her up and take care of her. It was liberating to not have to rely on her sitter (mainly my mom) to update me on important details like when my daughter took her first steps. I felt the liberty of enjoying my baby girl's earliest moments and capturing them in-person rather than waiting until my lunch break to call and check in.

Years down the road I had a second child, and add to that a homeschooling lifestyle, along with plenty of travel and three moves (one of which was cross country), and I admit to hitting quite a few bumps along the road as I was thrust into managing these aspects of my life. During certain life seasons, I was able to place my business on hold so that I could deal with the birth of a new baby or an upcoming big move. That is the beauty of the kind of flexibility that entrepreneurship brings women.

Another beautiful result of being a mompreneur is that your kids will oftentimes become your catalyst to business success. While many moms grumble and complain about not being able to get anything done with their kids around, there is something so very obvious about this season of your life that you cannot avoid: and it's the fact that you're a mother and your kids will ultimately need you at the most obvious and the most inopportune times. Since you cannot change this simple fact, why not make the best of this phase in life: morphing both your love for your work with your season of motherhood?

This is why I'm passionate. I love helping women awaken to the truth that your season of motherhood makes you even more gifted, talented, and able to succeed. I believe this because my season of awakening happened to me over ten years ago. It wasn't until I brought my first child into this world that I realized my potential for entrepreneurship, and it was because she was born that I felt motivated to leave the safety nest of my cozy job and take the risk to strike out on my own.

My daughter was my motivation, and every day that I worked on building my business while having her close by I knew that I was doing it all for her. Because her very presence motivated me, she pulled the best out of me-

and I found myself stretching beyond my limitations to prove that I could, in fact, recoup the salary I'd left back at my 9-5 office.

Yes, it took time, and no, this process wasn't an overnight one. I made some major sacrifices along the way, said no to daily coffee shop visits and a fancy wardrobe, ate out less and cooked more, and eventually stayed at home more often. My husband and I learned to live on one income as we put all of our hope and trust in God to keep our heads above water and pay our bills.

But with time, I began to see the benefits of owning and operating my own business where I set my own hours, set my own prices and delivered services that became my life passion. The fact that I could do all of this from the comfort of my home with nothing but a laptop and internet connection was superb.

Have you been dreaming of this lifestyle? Have you always wanted to lead a life of freedom to follow your dreams and explore your passions while increasing your financial leverage – not only for your family but for yourself?

If you answered yes to the above question, then I'm your gal. You are the reason I am writing this book. I'm here to help guide you to the road that best suits your particular entrepreneurial journey. Although your journey will be different from mine, I can give you some general starter points and guide you through the unique process of becoming a mompreneur- from vision to reality.

In this book, my aim is to help you:

- discover your money-making passion and potential
- position yourself for success by establishing a credible online presence
- attract the perfect customers for you

- develop an easy, yet fine-tuned blogging routine
- learn the keys to relationship-building through online networking
- balance your family life by getting them on board
- allow ample room for celebrating your successes

Each chapter in this book is intended to take you through the steps of beginning your online business successfully. I will cover everything from exposing your true passions (which may be neatly hidden or tucked away inside a label called "hobby"), to creating ongoing blogging routines that are easy for you to build into your everyday life, to celebrating the sale of your first service or product.

In this book (which I consider a DIY coaching series all right here in your hands!) you'll find a wide gamut of web success strategies. However, you'll also be able to easily follow along as I've strategically placed these steps in logical order. This step-by-step action plan will be your guide to bringing the mompreneur inside of you out into the open where you belong.

Are you ready for the journey? Go ahead and grab those mompreneur heels that have been hidden in your virtual closet for years, dig in, and let's start the course!

Chapter 2: Discover your passions.

What do you do first thing in the morning after a full night (or a half-night if you have small children) of sleep? If you're anything like me, you don't shoot out of bed bright-eyed and energetically announcing a cheerful morning call for a full course breakfast which you so graciously cooked for your entire family. (Although that wouldn't be such a bad idea). My point is, it takes a while to shake off the grogginess of sleep and to fully wake up. Coffee can help.

Although sleep is a recovery period for your body, waking up is a significant mode necessary for accomplishing your day's tasks and living a productive life. You have simply got to *wake up*.

Likewise, when you've been sleeping on your life vision, purpose, or passion for so long, it becomes a dream. Your dreams can only be dreamt about. A dream only becomes your reality once you wake up and begin living your purpose.

It's time to shake off the grogginess of your distant dream and awaken to your passion.

What is business passion?

So you're either wanting to start your online business and don't know where to begin, or you're thinking of rebranding your current business to make room for your passions. In other words, you want to blog about what you love and create a solid business structure online that supports you and your family financially. It all starts with passion.

Let's talk about your passions for a moment. Have you ever heard that so long as you're making money it doesn't matter if you love what you do or not?

Many business owners ascribe to ideologies that lead them to believe that tapping into their passions or purpose is futile. If you want to believe that, then you are free to go out and get a job- any job-and yes, you will make money. But there exists a breed of women (and men) out here who have taken our passions by the reigns and decided to do something about our purpose in life, turning our vision into reality and into multiple income streams.

We have decided that breaking beyond the cubicle barrier of the structured 9-5 workday was so important that we're willing to risk a little security in exchange for the freedom of being our own boss.

I absolutely LOVE being in control of my time- something that I had no control over when I worked a full-time job. There are many more reasons I love being an entrepreneur, but freedom plays a huge part in my decision. And I love having the freedom to create a business based on my passions.

What is passion, and why would you want to pursue it for business?

I love the way the Urban Dictionary puts it:

"Passion is when you put more energy into something than is required to do it. It is more than just enthusiasm or excitement; passion is ambition that is materialized into action to put as much heart, mind body and soul into

something as is possible."

This is precisely what you want for your business. Business passion means you are excited about your topic, enthusiastic about your goals and end result, and you're willing to put your heart, mind, body, and soul into it in order to see your project through to completion and keep your business running smoothly. Business passion means you love what you do. You don't just like it or tolerate it- you actually really, truly enjoy it.

Don't get me wrong: business is hard work. The ins and outs of running a business are critical and detail-intensive, but if you have the overall vision and purpose AND you're passionate about it, you can make your business idea work for you. With all the right pieces in place, the underlying essential ingredient for a successful business is passion.

It is my opinion that the bottom line isn't always money. You need passion and true belief in what you are doing in order to achieve the truest measure of success. Success goes so much further and deeper than your month's income (although your income has a huge part to play in success, of course!)

Bottom line: if you hate the day-to-day operations of your business, can't stand your clients and customers, and don't believe in your business products or services, you are not successful. Nobody wants to shop with a company that doesn't believe in what they offer and has poor customer service. The most successful companies are passionate about serving their clients and customers and are excited about their products and services. They are excited. They are passionate.

If you're just beginning this professional blogging journey, opening up your first online shop, or adding a virtual extension to your brick and mortar shop, you'll want to evaluate for the first time (or re-evaluate) your passions. Before you begin this journey of creating an online business, please take some time to ensure that you are absolutely ecstatic about your business idea. Otherwise, there could be some disappointing consequences. I want you to be excited so that your customers are as well.

If you're just starting out on this journey and have not created your blog yet, you are in a perfect place. Starting brand new is oftentimes easier than rebranding because you are starting with a clean slate and don't have a myriad of transitional issues to deal with. I know personally (as someone who has rebranded on several occasions) that it can be extremely difficult converting former clients to the new brand. It's far easier to know from Day 1 what it is we love to offer our clients and start out on the right foot.

At the beginning of this book, we'll explore three steps to starting your online business successfully: passion, purpose, and vision. Here's where it's time to get personal. If you're struggling with the desire to begin your business blog or rebrand your blog because you're unsure where to begin, let's go ahead and address the most important question:

WHAT IS *YOUR* BUSINESS PASSION?

I would like for you to take some time really reflect on this question. What could you see yourself doing for a living long term that you can truthfully commit to and love doing daily?

A business passion example:

I frequently visit a local coffee shop which has been around for nearly a decade. This mom and pop shop (owned and operated by a husband and wife team) gets raving reviews on Yelp for their friendliness and customer service. Although I don't dig the alternative rocker /Portland ambiance, my personal preference for cafe atmosphere is overruled by the friendly customer service. The owner truly gets his customers. He knows his regulars and what they'll order as they walk up to the counter. When he found out I was new in downtown San Jose, he gave me a brief overview of the hot spots in the area and welcomed me to the neighborhood. Oftentimes he is working the cafe all by himself with no assistance and single-handedly takes orders, works the espresso machine and wipes down tables all within a 10-minute time frame. And no telling how much time he takes behind the scenes working on his website and social media strategies. That takes some commitment.

This man wakes up every single morning to show up at his cafe and works to grow his business. He works hard and consistently, but he really seems to enjoy it.

Don't get me wrong- I realize life is not a bowl of fluff. I'm sure he's had his moments when life gets tough and it's hard to show up at the shop. I've heard that he's hit some rough patches with his son over the years. When you mix strained family relations with health problems and financial concerns, you could easily decide to give up on your business- unless, of course, you're so passionate about what you do that it's fulfilling enough for you to continue on, even through your hardships. Although, that's not to say we won't need temporary breaks or that we won't need to hit pause once in a while. When life deals you a rough hand, sometimes you have to put on the brakes and deal with your situation. But when or if you should decide to step back into the world of online business, hopefully your passion for what you do will be renewed and you will feel invigorated and ready to give it a second shot.

A MOMPRENEUR EXAMPLE

A good friend of mine began a blog geared toward a sector of the education market that had been nearly overlooked but is constantly growing larger. She spearheads a growing online community of African American homeschool moms.

As an African American mom *and* a homeschooling mom who understands the needs of this market, Andrea Thorpe began a website to address their needs. She also began a Facebook page that took off as quickly as she began it, climbing to over 1,000 members in less than 10 months! She is not only the moderator for her Facebook group as well as the founder and blogger of AfricanAmericanHomeschoolMoms.com, but she is also the founder, host, and coordinator of the African American Homeschool Moms Conference, (a face to face, offline event) which she began hosting in 2015 in the New Jersey area.

As a result of Andrea's persistence with establishing credible authority in her niche with a blog (her home base), a strong social media presence (her Facebook group), and a strong local presence (her homeschool conference), she was able to establish her brand and her authority in the topic within a short amount of time. I find Andrea a great example of a mom with a passion who was able to create a community of influence as a result.

Back to you!

So, by now you should feel encouraged and motivated. Others have done this and you can too. So, do you have a business idea in mind yet?

If you still don't have a clue, let me give you a huge hint:

your hobbies!

If you spend a lot of time knitting, creating your own lesson plans, designing graphic headers for blogs, or enjoy sharing your fashion with others- and especially if you are already blogging about your hobby- please don't forget to take your hobby into consideration as a passion. Your hobbies are oftentimes the hidden gems to a lucrative blog. Many moms and women in business have built successful businesses by taking a former hobby and turning it into cash.

And yet another idea: **your interests.**

What types of books and magazines do you gravitate toward in bookstores? If you were in Barnes and Noble or your local library, which sections of the store or library would you make a beeline toward? What are your favorite non-fiction titles?

Do you listen to podcasts? Do you watch documentaries on Netflix? What are some of the topics that interest you the most?

And lastly: **your conversations.**

What do you talk about most frequently with your friends and family? What lights your fire? What are your aspirations? When you're in "I wish" status and your friends catch you with that dreamy look on your face, what is your topic of discussion?

Usually for a budding entrepreneur, there will be that one topic that you just can't seem to sit on. You could talk about it for hours and days. Unless you're super quiet about it, your friends and family will be able to tell you what your passions are. If you're still unsure what they are, just ask them.

You'll need this kind of passion in order to capitalize on the gifts and talents that were given to you. I believe that every individual was born with a unique set of gifts and that they were given to us so that we can, in turn, give them back to the world in which we live. You see, people need you and your gifts. They need what you have so that they can be more complete. If you withhold your gifts, you are doing your clients and customers a disservice.

Another word of advice: **don't mistake gifts and talents for perfectionism or super genius abilities.** Although you might be a genius, the majority of us don't feel we compare to Einstein, and that's okay. The truth is, there is a little bit of genius in everyone. In fact, if we truly tap into our creative genius, there is actually quite a lot of it. The more we tap in, the more we find. You might have an uncanny knack for something, a skill, a unique ability that you might find particularly easy that perhaps your friend finds extremely difficult. This is your genius. This is the one thing that, combined with passion, could blow your online business off the roof!

It's okay if you're unable to locate that one gift or talent in this particular exercise. I just want you to be aware that you do possess it. It could come in a variety of forms. Sometimes it looks like an ability. Sometimes it looks like a performance. Sometimes it just looks like an everyday, ordinary task that, when compared to others, you simply shine in that area.

What is it that you love to do? What is it that you desire to do- even if you haven't quite figured out how you'll accomplish it yet? What is it that you have been putting on hold for such a long time now? How can I help you transition from lacing up your sneakers to eventually slipping on those mompreneur heels?

My proposal to you is that we take a look at your current

situation and analyze where you are today, then figure out a roadmap to where you need to be. This will be different for each individual, so it's totally okay that your path looks completely different than mine. In fact, it should look different than mine.

I always ask my clients to really begin to reflect on their past and present in order to understand their future. You'll have to understand how you got to the point where you are today in order to make the necessary changes for a life detour. Don't worry- you are not jumping off a cliff, just taking a simple detour in your path. This detour, as we call it, is only healthy for you if you know without a doubt that entrepreneurship is for you. I take it the reason you are reading this book is because you are desperate to shift your life in a direction that feels more meaningful to you.

So, let's dig right in and begin with a crucial assessment that will get your wheels turning about your passions in life.

Gifts and talents assessment

It is my firm belief that every human being was born with some innate gifting. As I mentioned earlier, it doesn't mean that everybody is an Einstein, but everybody on earth certainly has a bit of genius within. The human capacity is much greater than we could ever imagine. (Did you realize that our brains have unchartered territories that throughout our lifetime will go undiscovered and unused simply because we never created opportunity for the brain to work in a greater capacity?)

Certainly we are not meant to accomplish everything, nor should we attempt to achieve perfection or stretch ourselves beyond what we're meant to. But a slight stretch to reach the next level of your life will be necessary as you begin to shift your mindset and think like a mompreneur.

If you've been a Debbie Downer when it comes to your abilities, gifts, talents, and passions, then you need to drop the victim attitude right away in order to find success. In the beginning, I'm very patient with my clients who tell me "I want to be a mompreneur, but I have absolutely nothing to offer." But after we sit down and begin to really drill down into their passions and their aspirations, I don't give room for excuses. I know that sounds tough, but it's the only way to pave the path out of monotony into the freedom you want. Success breeds success. The more positive you are that your offerings to the world are worthy of your future customers' time and money, the more confident you'll be to pursue the business you've been dreaming of, and actually make it happen.

You know why I can be a little tough? Because I've been in that place where I didn't feel like what I had to offer was good enough. Despite the fact that I always had a billion projects up my sleeve- many of which I could do pretty well if I tried- I somehow always ended up feeling like my attempts at them were short-lived or futile. Over the past decade, I've begun many web projects, which I've scrapped after only a few tries. I've begun over three businesses- only one of which has proven successful enough for me to justify the time I spent building it. I tell you all of this to secure your trust that I understand exactly what it takes to pull yourself up out of the pit and keep going.

Finally, after many false attempts and after much trial and error, I was able to begin building a business that I love- not just because it was another great money-making idea, but because I finally understood what it meant to capitalize on my gifts and my passions.

In order to help you avoid some of the pitfalls I fell into while hopping on a variety of different business ideas that I wasn't passionate about at all, I'd like for you to take a few moments to answer the following questions to help you toward determining your unique gifts. Remember, a gift or talent is not indicative of Einstein-like genius (although I like to call all mompreneurs geniuses), but rather is simply a natural aptitude or skill. If you have a knack for something, a touch, a bent, or even a hint of expertise, then you're on to something. You have a gift. I prefer to coach you through starting your business by tapping into your natural abilities because you are more likely to be successful at operating a business in which you are passionate about the topic.

Let's not rule out your hobbies. If you spend a lot of time knitting, creating your own lesson plans, designing graphic headers for blogs, or enjoy sharing your fashion with others- and especially if you are already blogging about your hobby- please don't forsake to highly take your hobby into consideration as a passion. Again, many moms have built successful businesses by taking a former hobby and turning it into cash.

So for now- grab a notebook and pen, let's begin the discovery of your talents and gifts.

What is your current position?

In order to figure out where you are going, you must take an assessment of where you are today. Just like planning a road trip, you need to know not only your destination but your current position in relation to where you are going. Only then can you plot out an easy path to arrive at your final destination.

Where you are today doesn't determine your tomorrow- but I would like for you to write down your place in the entrepreneurial journey on today.

Ask yourself: are you at the very beginning or closer to the middle of the road?

What are your current positions and jobs in life today? Don't leave out anything. Do you volunteer at your church or your child's school? Do you knit hats and donate them to children's hospitals? Are you a budding artist? Maybe you love teaching your nieces/ daughters/grandchildren to dance. Do you enjoy helping adults learn to read, or cooking meals? If you work, what do you do at your current job? Everything counts- so be sure to not leave out anything.

What do you absolutely LOVE to do in your current position?

Whether you're a life coach, an author, a speaker, or a stay at home mom- there is something you are doing today that you most likely wouldn't mind doing long term, especially if you were paid well for it.

Really think this section through, then write down the things you enjoy doing most.

What are your hobbies and interests?

Whether you have the opportunity to do these things regularly or not, definitely include your interests. Hobbies have been known to jumpstart many businesses for mompreneurs, so never discount an interest that you maybe work on occasionally.

What types of books and magazines do you like to read?

This exercise will most likely get you on the road to discovery of your interests fairly quickly. Among your list of non-fiction books and favorite magazines, which titles do you love the most? Which section of a bookstore would you spend most of your time in?

- DIY
- Parenting
- Health
- Spirituality
- Education
- Business
- Crafts
- Fashion
- Other

Which online websites/blogs do you frequent the most?

In my spare time, I always enjoy visiting blogs and keeping up with my favorites. The type of blogs you follow may indicate some of your interest level in the topics you've chosen to keep up with. Blogs are a great way to discover your hidden interests. If you enjoy reading what others are blogging about a topic, there's a high chance you are interested in that topic!

Do you subscribe to any podcasts or video channels?

Name the topics discussed on these audio and video outlets that you enjoy consuming. Again, this is another sure-fire way to discover some of your hidden interests. Scroll through the Itunes store and browse the podcast listings to see what strikes your fancy. Traipse on over to YouTube and see which videos you are attracted to. You might just be surprised at your selections. You may discover interests you never knew you had.

What do you talk about most often?

If you're not sure how to answer this one, just ask your family or friends. I guarantee they'll know!

What do you believe is your gift to the world?

Whether you're operating in your true gift or not, what do you think your purpose is in life? You can have more than one answer.

And lastly, two BIG questions for mompreneurs:

Working Moms: *If you could quit your current job or decrease your work hours while making more money, and you could choose to do anything in the world, what would you do?*

At-Home Moms: *If you could squeeze in any activity between the hours that you're parenting your kids, what would you most like to work on?*

Let your heart do the talking! Again, you may have more than one answer.

Now that you have analyzed your current position, what do you think? Where are you exactly in your discovery of your gifts and talents? Have you picked up on some clues about what type of business you want to pursue?

Whether you have discovered that you constantly check out books about travel or that you read a barrage of magazines about parenting, has this exercise helped you to see that your interests can be a window of discovery- leading you to your passions?

I'm a firm believer that your passions and interests can oftentimes lead you into your life's purpose. In this lifetime you will have several purposes in which your family and your community are touched by your presence. Your purpose will serve the world around you in a variety of different ways at different times and involve different functions. But many times, it all starts with a passion.

Once you tap into your passion, my friend, you're on your way to successful blogging- the cornerstone for your online business.

Before you begin the next leg of the journey, I would like for you to continue to discover your interests until you've narrowed down your list and have chosen one topic that will be your main web project- the crux of your business. Don't overanalyze this exercise. It doesn't have to be a perfect choice. Just be sure to select the one topic that you could talk about- a LOT. You don't even have to know much about it just yet. Developing expertise will come with time. You just need to be attracted to it and be willing to learn more about it. Better still, if you feel that you have a certain knack for it- a talent or gift, if you will- it could make your business so much more effective.

Remember, we're talking in terms of **creating an online business through blogging**. In order to make money at blogging successfully, you don't need the most brilliant idea, a ton of startup cash, and a garage full of inventory. All you need is a credible idea that lends itself toward your passions, a few online business essentials (which we'll get into later on in the book), and a forward-thinking, purpose-driven attitude.

So what's holding you back? Hopefully, nothing at this point. Let's continue through our action step guide to the next chapter, where I will address a few things that can hold you back from taking additional steps in your entrepreneurial journey. We'll knock that out of the way and then continue on to begin your idea research.

Chapter 3: Overcoming Business Fears

We all deal with fear, and for whatever reason, fear seems to appear the most when you're making an attempt to do something extremely important in your life.

Any number of situations can cause you to be afraid to take your first step into entrepreneurship. Maybe you're currently working a full- time or part-time job and you're unsure about how to ease out of your current job and come home while maintaining a sustainable nest egg and income.

Perhaps you've been out of the workforce for years and you're really uncertain how to go about dipping your toes into the waters again. And maybe you've never truly held down a job or even started a business before. If this is your first time striking out on your own, no doubt it's a scary situation.

Moms come from all different backgrounds, and I completely understand that no two situations are alike. The advice in this book is for all moms who have the drive and passion to change her current situation, reach for her dreams, and make a difference for herself and her family.

However, many times with the responsibility of change comes fear. If you are having issues with overcoming business fears, know that you're not alone. Here are a few tips that have helped me to get past my fears of becoming more visible online through video and podcasting, to push myself out there in the world of online business, and begin making connections.

Tip 1: Accept yourself for who you are.

It's really, totally okay to be you. Love and embrace yourself, then you won't have any problems showing the world who you are. Loving yourself just means being familiar with and accepting of your gifts and talents. You should also expect that your tribe will love you back. Not everyone will love what you do, but you will make a significant impact on those to whom you are meant to serve, and they will be faithful to your brand.

Tip 2: Get out of your "you" zone and into your "others" zone.

Remember that people need what you offer. You must know that what you have to offer is valuable. It's not about what you don't think you're good at it- it's what others need from you. What do you have that you can offer to those around you? Take this question and make it your business motto. What can you offer your customers and clients that come straight from your heart to theirs? Allow your new work to become your service to your clients. This is where it's not about you any longer, but about your prospects.

Tip 3: Be willing to take a chance on the uncomfortable.

Again, building a business is not a comfortable place to be. Remember, you're building from the ground up- so there will definitely be some sweat and tears in the process. You will oftentimes feel like hiding behind a rock rather than getting up to speak in front of a live audience. You might feel the fear of beginning to do videos or podcasts or becoming public in social media. Initially, you might even feel a tremendous amount of fear just stepping out to begin your blog. It's understandable. You're taking a huge leap of faith and putting your reputation on the line- so, yes, it's uncomfortable. On the flip side, the more you blog, the more you speak in front of audiences, and the more you create videos or podcasts or tweet about your blog, the easier it all becomes.

Tip 4: Quit comparing yourself to other business owners.

Oh my word- is this ever a big no-no in my book. You just can't compare yourself to anyone else. The other woman business owner who you think may have it all together might have some situations worked out for her behind the scenes that you have no clue about. Maybe she has a nanny or a housekeeper which explains the super clean home and the extra time she has to work more on her business. Maybe her husband watches the kids while she works three days out of the week, or she's arranged for child care 5 hours per day. You just don't know. If you don't have those amenities, your life will, of course, function differently and you will make arrangements as needed for your own business. The woman that you think has it all together (gets all her blog posts planned out months in advance, has clients on a mile-long waiting list, travels first-class every month to fancy dinners with prospective clients) may very well be struggling with managing things on the home front. She might even somewhat envy the mompreneur who seems to have more time to cuddle with her baby. So you see, it's really not fair to compare apples to oranges.

Tip 5: Take action!

Procrastination is the enemy of success. If you want to self-sabotage your business quickly, procrastinating is the number one way to do that. As women, many of us tend to second-guess ourselves over and over again. We make a decision to do something, and then we begin to look around and notice that no one else is doing it quite the same. Rather than feeling like the odd one out, and afraid that we'll appear silly, we immediately renege and decide to hold back on our decision. I've done it a time or two. In fact, getting this book written and published lingered on and on for over a year. I had my laptop stolen (on which this book's draft was saved) and thought I'd lost the book forever. Then I realized it was in Dropbox and I still had a chance. Save! What grace. So I had no excuses. I had to keep going until the work was complete.

Another thing we may tend to do, in addition to avoiding standing out like a sore thumb, is over-researching an idea to death. Once you have a really good idea- let me give you a huge hint here: GO FOR IT!!! If you don't take action on it, someone else will likely get the same idea and will go for it. So why not you?

What's holding you back?

Take a few moments to answer the following questions. Write down all of your fears about business while answering these two questions about each:

What am I afraid of?

Why am I afraid?

What steps will you take to overcome your fears of beginning an online business? Once you complete this exercise, you'll have a better idea of what is holding you back from moving forward in your decision to start your business blog.

Over the past decade, I've listened to many moms tell me how they would like to start an online business but are afraid they won't be able to learn to blog effectively, or that they don't have the money, or they're worried about looking foolish if it all fizzles.

These are all legitimate concerns. In fact, I still feel that way every time I branch out into something new. For example, I have created online courses before, but very soon after this book is published I will be venturing into unknown territory: membership sites. At the moment of writing this book, creating a membership site appears pretty daunting to me. There is also a certain amount of fear about things going wrong. I have my share of "what-if" moments and, like many Type A moms, I tend to overanalyze, over-research, and over-plan. Knowing this about myself gives me the opportunity to catch myself in those weak moments and pull back briefly. Whenever I start to worry that I might not be able to accomplish that project I'm setting out to do, I start to ask myself these same questions. I ask myself "What am I afraid of?" and "Why am I afraid?"

I've come to the conclusion that there are two key ways to deal with fear in order for you to free up yourself to move forward.

1. **You can stare fear in the face and plunge into your project full throttle**! Risky, yes- but absolutely exhilarating. Once you jump in there's no turning back. These kinds of mompreneurs will purchase a domain, hire a designer, build a team, and start blogging in one fell swoop. Some people thrive off this adrenaline-rush incentivizing to get moving. Others of us need to take things nice and slow.

2. **You can gradually ease into your online business** by doing less in the beginning, taking your time, and working

with one new concept at a time. This could mean focusing on learning one new skill at a time. If it's blogging, you simply focus on finding a rhythm in your daily routine to blog, or pulling together a list of blog topics. The point is, finding one simple task and focusing on only that one thing can simplify the experience for you and lessen the fear.

Once you've effectively dealt with the fear, then you are more capable of taking a position and setting the stage for your business success.

Chapter 4: Research

Positioning Yourself

I'm excited for you! At this point, you've discovered a few business ideas that you would like to pursue based on your interests- either for the first time or yet another time around for a rebrand. In this chapter, we'll uncover what it means to **get into position.**

Preparation is key for any event that happens in your life. Whether you're getting married, moving to a new state, or your kids are heading off to college, you've likely already begun preparing for these big events in your life.

I'm not sure why starting up an internet business seems like an afterthought to many (which is why their online businesses fail, by the way), but throwing together an awkward blog and hoping on a whim that it attracts enough attention to make a few sales here and there is not the way to go. If you're going into this to make money, then let's treat your project like a business.

Here are some scenarios just to make this really hit home for you:

Before you purchase a car, you do a little research, shop around, compare prices, and make sure you're getting a good deal, right?

When you first set out to buy a house, you make sure that your finances are in order and if there are any outstanding debts you work hard to get those minimized. Then, you scout the territory: figure out the exact location you want to live, weigh the pros and cons of moving into that area, lay out a list of must-haves for your new dwelling place, and begin asking the locals about their experience living there. The point is, a lot of research goes into buying a new home.

It's absolutely the same with building a business. Rather than a brick and mortar shop, you're setting up shop virtually with your blog. Your blog is now your storefront and your business landscape is online.

Before you "move in" to your new virtual real estate, you'll want to take inventory by asking questions about the area and finding out what kind of businesses are already setting up shop nearby. It's always a good idea to look around and see who your healthy competition is because you will be able to find out so much by what's already out there. You'll also want to make sure you have a viable business idea by narrowing down your target market and checking to make sure your chosen blog topic is being searched for daily by your potential customers.

Here's what we'll do now. By this point, you must have discovered a few important facts about your likes and dislikes. More importantly, you have pinpointed a number of ideals, favorite activities, hobbies, and interests. You have your business idea in mind and you're ready to get started with some viable research to set up your business successfully online.

We'll be making good use of a simple strategy called **keyword research**. Now, don't let this scare you. Though I don't claim to be an internet marketing guru by any means, I've studied under quite a few in the past decade. Although search engine algorithms have changed over the years, the basic premise of marketing online has not. My goal is to simplify the process for you so that you don't have to worry about a lot of technical or guru marketing jargon. Although if you want more, I can definitely point you to some great resources for specifics.

Keyword Research

So what is this keyword research all about?

First off, your business is online- so you'll need to think about setting your blog foundation virtually, much like you would think of securing a proper venue if you had a brick and mortar business. Remember, it's all about location, location, location. Just because your business happens to be virtual, doesn't mean that location doesn't matter.

Your location- when online- refers to where your online presence is visible. Where do people find your site? How are you visible? Where are you visible? **Are** you visible?

That's where keywords come in handy.

If you want to be found naturally (through organic search engine results), you'll need to be thinking of a few keywords that will be a focus on your blog. This, of course, will tie into the theme of your business and will become a seamless process. But you've got to start somewhere, and a handful of good keywords will take you far in the digital world.

What is an organic search engine result?

Here is the easiest way I can explain this:

Let's pretend you've just had a baby recently. If your kids are mostly grown up, stretch your imagination with me, if you will!

If you're totally into cloth diapering and co-sleeping, you might be interested in finding a really good sling. What are the best brands? You need something secure, versatile, easy to wear, comfy for baby, and trendy. So you google "baby slings".

The first five results in the search engine become your campout for the next half hour as you scour each of those sites for the exact sling you're looking for. One of those five sites makes it to your favorites list, and after you bookmark the site you proceed to add one of their slings to your shopping cart and follow through with a purchase. You also make sure to add your name to their mailing list to be sure you stay notified of any discounts and store news for future purchases. Additionally, you decide to follow them on twitter and forward the company info on Facebook to a friend of yours who is also looking for slings.

All of these connections with this one company resulted from your **one search in Google**. If this babywear company hadn't purchased any network ads, the reason you found their site in such a high position on the search engine results page is because they leveraged the power of keywords. By strategically using the keywords they knew customers like you would use in order to find them in Google, they were able to rise to the top of the search engine results and land your purchase!

This is what I want to help you learn to do- quickly and simply. As I mentioned before, keyword research is a science that changes with the algorithms of Google or Bing- so it can become quite complex if you want to go down that road. I don't. I want this to be a simple process, and that's what I aim to show you.

Just know that when it comes to keyword research, you'll get a variety of differing opinions. Talk to a number of different internet marketers and you'll get a host of answers when it comes to answering the main questions like what characteristics to look for in the best keywords, how many searches a good keyword should have, or whether or not to purchase a domain based on your keyword.

Since I won't be covering keyword research in depth here, I just want to ease your worries about it by informing you of a simple (and free) tool that can help you gather a very general idea about selecting a good keyword.

Again, my focus here is not to bore you with the details of analytics or cause you to go into reverse in your business planning because the keyword research seemed complicated. If you're the type that loves to dig into the nuts and bolts of keyword research and analytics, I'll be more than happy to work with you in person, but for the purpose of this book, let's make it short and sweet.

The tool:

Google Keyword planner is a wonderful choice for a keyword analytics tool.

The long and short of it is, you should select a blog topic that gets a relatively good amount of searches each month. The number of searches will vary and will depend on your topic. Don't overanalyze, but again, we want to be sure that there are at least some people looking for some information related to your brilliant business idea!

The gist of keyword research:

When researching keywords, your main idea is to run your keyword through Google Keyword Planner as a filter. You want to see the competition (how many other sites are using the same keyword) as well as how many searches are made within your geographic area. The tighter this ratio, the easier it will be for you to gain traffic to your blog organically on search engines.

The How-To:

First things first. To get to Keyword Planner, visit this link: https://adwords.google.com/

Go ahead and create an account if you don't have one already.

Navigate over to "tools", then click on "Keyword Planner". Your screen should look similar to this:

At this point, go to "Search for new keyword and ad group ideas".

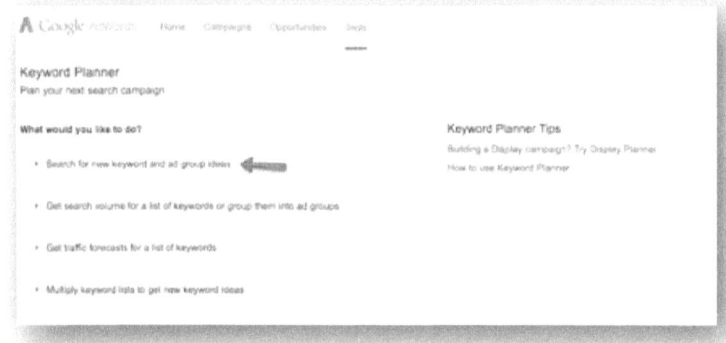

Type in your keyword idea. For example, if you're an independent book publisher, you can type in "book publishers".

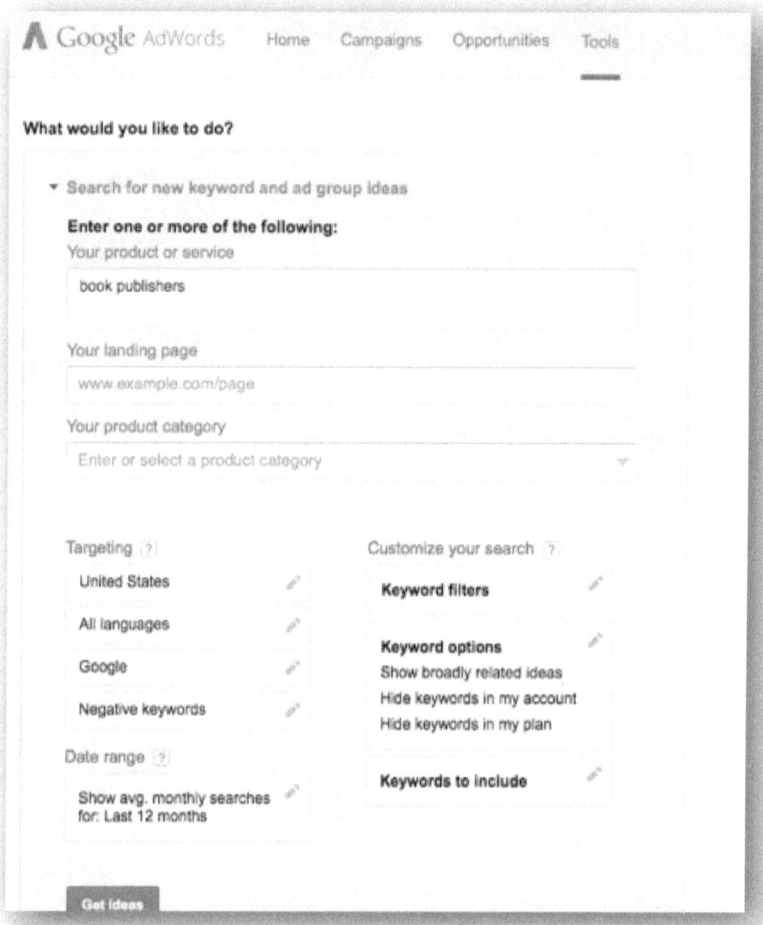

Click "get ideas". Click on the sub-tab "keyword ideas". As you can see, at one glance you'll notice a few important details about your book publishing business idea. Specifically, the keyword "book publishers".

At the time I'm searching this, competition is high for this word although average monthly searches sit pretty decent, at 5,400 searches per month.

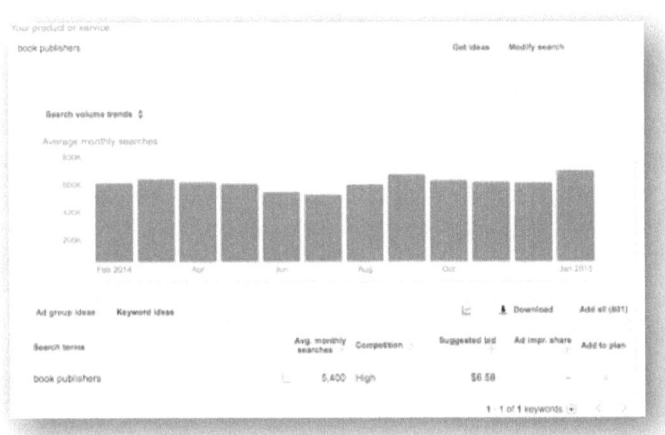

If you look at a few other variations such as "book publishing" or "book publishing companies" the results are about the same, with high competition and in some cases, even slightly lower searches per month.

Your goal is to find keywords related to your business that have a high demand of searches combined with lower competition. This perfect combination will set your blog up for success from the very beginning, by offering your business the opportunity to outrank many similar online businesses simply by having a more optimized blog for search engines.

SEO (search engine optimization) is important even at the earliest stage.

And remember, the success of your blog does not entirely depend on your domain name choice. A good keyword is helpful in giving you organic ranking but is definitely not the only factor in a successful blog.

My encouragement to you is- when it comes to keywords, find a handful of good ones with low to medium competition range and which will garner you a nice amount of traffic monthly. Use these keywords as anchors throughout your blog.

For example, in the book publishing instance, look for some variations on the "book publishers" keyword and coin other ideas related to publishing books that may give you the searches. In the sample below, I typed in "how to publish a book". If you scroll down to view all the results, you'll find that you can also sort by competition. Sort it from low to high so that you can get your hands on the least competitive keywords, and keep your eyes peeled for the higher numbers for average monthly searches.

Now, there are bound to be some results that are irrelevant to your business. But what if you find a few gold nuggets in the batch?

Let's say you're interested in sharing information to help your clients publish book reviews. Look at the "book review format" keyword and its monthly search result indicated at the purple arrow.

Keyword (by relevance)	Avg. monthly searches	Competition	Suggested bid	Ad impr. share	Add to plan
how to publish a book					
how to get started writing	90	Low	–	–	–
first book published	50	Low	–	–	–
how to write your story	70	Low	–	–	–
short story writer	90	Low	$4.26	–	–
book review format	880	Low	$0.63	–	–
how to be entrepreneur	90	Low	$2.44	–	–
ape book	70	Low	$2.49	–	–
your novel	90	Low	$4.57	–	–

The number 880 may not seem like much, but you'll notice that compared to the 50, 70, and 90 searches for other keywords in comparison, 880 is much more. In fact, close to 1,000 searches per month on a keyword is not all that bad. Of course, the more the better- but 1,000 is a great start. Not only is this keyword receiving close to a thousand searches this past month, but it has a low competition rate. This means that you have an open avenue on your website to use this keyword effectively throughout your content and pull in some organic clicks. Your site will likely rank higher for this specific keyword over and above other websites, if you use this keyword throughout the body, title, meta tags, and images of your blog posts. (I'll explain all this in more detail later on.)

You won't need to use this keyword on every single page unless your entire blog is about book review formats. Just a few blog posts may do the trick. However, if you aim to be the #1 go-to source for self-publishing, you'll definitely want to find a keyword that indicates your objective, and use it liberally throughout your blog -within reason, of course! No keyword stuffing! (Keyword stuffing is simply sticking a selected keyword throughout the body of your content repeatedly, even when it makes no sense, in an attempt to hijack search engines so you get a higher ranking. Hey, I know you wouldn't do anything like that- but I should probably just mention it. Search engines are much smarter these days in detecting unrealistic blog posts and articles.)

So now your job is to come up with a handful of keywords related to your business. Go ahead and play around with Keyword Planner. Get familiar with keyword-hunting because it can help you tremendously in finding ideas to blog about long-term in addition to helping you find anchor keywords for your business idea! Once your blog is launched and you're ready to begin your blogging strategy, you'll most likely return to Keyword Planner for ideas and for popular search phrases.

When you have these keywords, you can rest assure that your business idea is lucrative enough to begin setting up virtual shop.

That's pretty much the gist of keyword research. Again, as I mentioned before, you can contact me for more information on how to dig even deeper if you're interested. For now, I just want you to have a handful of keywords at your fingertips that you think will be helpful for your business. Use these throughout your blogging process.

Later on in the book, I will get into the details of how to sell your expertise online. My assumption is that at this point you will have determined what it is you want to sell and that you are preparing your product or service for sale. Please don't move on and purchase your domain name until you know for sure what you're planning to sell.

So- you ready? Okay, later on, I promise, I'll discuss all the important things like determining your company vision, purpose, and branding. And we'll get into more specifics about selling your products online. But for now, let's jump right into purchasing domain names.

Purchasing your domain name

Okay, this is the fun part. This is fun because I've done it more than a dozen times. I promise you, each time is more fun than the last!

I see domain-purchasing the way I do investing in real estate. My domain name is my virtual real estate and my $9.99 investment (sometimes $1.99 at GoDaddy) makes me thousands of dollars. But I don't take this investment lightly. That's why I made such a big deal about keyword research. Invest carefully.

When you purchase a domain name, you are buying the power of your brand. What do you want to be known as? How do you want to be perceived? All of this will transpire through your domain name, as you'll be using it all the time- on your business cards and all of your marketing materials.

Here are some key must-haves for choosing your domain name:

It must be easy to pronounce and spell. This goes without saying. If it's a mouthful to get out, it probably won't go over well. Make it simple and easy to remember. Spelling also counts, too. Remember, if someone hears your website domain on a radio announcement or podcast, you'll want them to be able to remember how to spell it (and pronounce it.)

Leave out dashes. If possible, try to get a first level domain with no dashes or hyphens. One of my first business sites which I no longer own was www.faith-media.com. The hyphen was a pain to explain on each of my podcasts, and it would have been so much easier to simply point everyone to "faith media dot com". Instead, I had to always remember to pronounce the hyphen, just in case those listening were not at their computers and needed to remember for later.

Now, if you have a special domain name that you simply have to have, but an unhyphenated version is not available, by all means- grab the one with the dash. Search engines are still very friendly toward them, and as far as I know there are no penalties for hyphenated domains. (In fact, there are arguments in favor of using dashes.) It really is all about preference, so do what feels more natural for your business.

The shorter, the sweeter. Yes, the domain name should probably be short and sweet. Again, it's all about helping your prospects find you easier. Typing in a simple 1 to 3-word domain name is a lot easier (and quicker) than typing in a long 4-5 word URL. You just have to think about mechanics.

Take advantage of keywords. Okay, here's the good thing about your keyword selections and why it's so important to choose good ones. When you select a domain name that has your keyword in it, you are off to a wonderful start so far as SEO goes. Anything for a great start, right?

Again, using the example of a book publisher, if you can find a domain name with "book publisher" as part of it, you've already set up your blog to be anchored around that keyword on **every page**. This is huge!

In this case, hyphenated or not, long or short, the fact that your keyword is part of your URL can be a major player for influencing your blog's credibility as an authority on the topic. So locate those keywords and think about which one would make a great domain name.

Now, if you're just itching to use your own name for your URL or the name of your business (which doesn't use any of your keyword selections), then no worries. It really isn't a big deal. At the end of the day, your domain name doesn't necessarily have to have your keyword in it to make a keyword and content-rich blog, but in my opinion, every little bit helps.

So now, you've thought about your domain name, you're ready to find a really good one and make the purchase. I will share with you one of my favorite hot spots for purchasing domain names and how it all works.

Buying a domain name

There are a number of domain name companies out there. Just do a quick Google search and take your pick, but I've used GoDaddy. Another suggestion is Namecheap.com or Siteground.com. Oftentimes you can find pretty nice coupon deals on first-time domain purchases for less than $2.00 for the first year. Of course, annual renewals will price out around $10-$15 which is pretty average for a typical domain name.

When buying a domain name, you'll first need to search to make sure it's available. So if you're new to this, go ahead and create an account, then do a quick search for your domain.

Click on "Domain Search" underneath "Find a Domain" and type in your desired domain address. If it's available, snatch it up right away. If not, then play around with some different variations of it. Contrary to my earlier advice, if you choose to use a hyphen but you still get those much-desired keywords in your domain, go right ahead and grab it. Maybe try adding a word or switching the words around a bit.

So, for instance, if you want to keep the key phrase "book publisher" in your domain, your first choice would be to, of course, search for bookpublisher.com. However, it's taken.

So, what next?

In this case, you could either select from the suggestions listed (which consist of extensions like .pub, .net, .org, .info and the like. But if you're not satisfied with these and really want that dot com extension (which I recommend), then try adding a word or two.

Adding in "nifty" at the beginning of the URL changed things! And so did the word "tutor" at the end of the URL.

In these instances, we simply added an extra word, either at the beginning or the end of your keyword phrase "book publisher"- and voila! You have a domain name using your chosen keyword- plus, it's available! How's that for nifty?

GATHERING YOUR IDEAS THROUGH IDEA JOURNALING

Whew! You've just purchased your domain name! Congratulations. It was a lot of work and research, but it was time well worth spent. You are on the road to an exciting journey of adventure and discovery. Now that you have the research aspect of your blog idea set in place you should feel confident about your business idea. (Remember your business and your blog are one and the same, and I'll be using these terms interchangeably throughout this book.)

There are some major steps toward going from your domain purchase to having an active blog filled with life, activity, and money-making adrenaline- but before we get on that freeway, let's take some more time to journey slowly through your ideas. We're not completely out of the woods yet!

Your next steps will encompass setting up your blog (having it designed, setting up your technology, learning to use WordPress- oh, and a whole lot more). But don't worry. I've got your back. This book covers it all, and I am dedicated to helping you step by step through this system.

Before we jump into the technology of it all, you should take some time think through how you want your blog to flow. What I mean by this is: your blog needs to have a blueprint in place. Rome wasn't built in a day- and I'm sure the architects of the time knew exactly how they envisioned Rome should be built. In contrast, your business blog might just be built in a few days. However, similar to Rome's construction, you've got to be the Master architect and create the blueprint for the overall vision of your blog design and setup.

This means thinking through your blog topics and categories. It means visualizing how you plan to interact within the context of your blog to your audience. It means thinking through how your audience may interact with you through your blog. And mostly, it means thinking through how you will exchange goods and services for money- your source of income.

In a later chapter, we'll discuss purpose and vision in more detail since this is an extremely important feature of your business blog. Without vision and purpose, you don't have much going-power. But for now, I'll just assume you have a general idea of your purpose and where you want to go with your blog. I'll also assume that you have some general idea of the topics you'd like to cover on your blog.

So, for now, your assignment is to carve out some time in your already-busy day and sketch out the future of your blog. Remember, the setup process- like any other task- is a bit more work in the beginning, but it's so worth it! What you'll end up with is a blog that speaks volumes of your vision for your company and what you offer to the world. You are in charge here, and the ball is in your court.

For this assignment, you don't need to consult Keyword

Planner. Those keyword ideas are for later when you actually start blogging. For now, you are thinking in terms of the Big Picture. If we go back to the example of the book publisher, you might envision how a book publisher would shape her blog.

She might start with the general info, like "how will a customer contact me?" and "how will they find my blog posts" to more specific questions like "what types of content will they want to read about on my blog and how will I organize this content?" With these questions in mind, she'll want to sketch out a framework for her blog.

Here's an example of how a book publisher might begin formulating ideas for her blog.

Blog Design Plan

Top Navigation: Home
Main Navigation Menu: Writing | Design| Printing |Self-publishing | Marketing
Color Theme: Sky Blue/Magenta
Template Layout: 2-column

Home Page

Top Navigation → Home	About	Contact| Consult| Podcast	
Main Navigation → Writing	Design: Printing |Self-publishing	Marketing	
	SIDEBAR
Slider or Introductory blog Info/ Splash Page	Book A Free Consult Button
	Podcast Button
Recent Blog entries	
	Ads Here
Footer	

As you can see, the blogging ideas are well thought-out, as well as what might end up being her layout for the blog. Figuring out her navigation menu items allows her the opportunity to think through some topics she will commit to blogging about and gives her a focus. Thinking through site colors, logo placement, and layout is extremely helpful.

Especially important is that she has decided on her main subtopics for the blog. In this instance, she'll be writing about marketing, self-publishing, design, and writing, and possibly even offering some or all of these services. Having a blogging plan of action from the very beginning is extremely important. (And for the sake of it, I have to add here that whatever you choose for your blog subtopics, make sure you like writing about it! In order to have a successful blog, you need to actually enjoy writing about your topic of choice.)

I encourage you to really begin thinking through the process here and don't skimp on anything. Your idea journaling is beginning to take shape and form and will be a foundation for you as you approach the "build" stage, coming up in the next chapter. In fact, you're more than halfway done with this stage as you've already begun sketching your outline, layout, and framework for your blog. You've already got a massive head start.

In this chapter, I hope you see how that using tools such as Keyword Planner, educating yourself about keyword research, purchasing your domain, sketching an outline of your blog, and idea journaling can all help you to get into position for building a successful blog. In the next chapter, we'll get into some nuts and bolts of the behind-the-scenes technology that make your blog run, and how to set it all up.

Chapter 5: Set up a beautifully successful blog.

Designing Your Blog

Are you ready to set up your blog? If you've already designed and your business rebrand doesn't include a re-do of your blog, then you can safely skip this section. However, I recommend you read through it anyway since most rebrands will require some redesign and restructuring of your current website. If this is your first time setting up a blog or you otherwise feel like a newbie regarding blog design, then this chapter is for you, my friend!

Welcome to one of the most exciting aspects of online business building for mompreneurs: designing and setting up your virtual shop! I LOVE this part of the process- even though at times it can feel like one of the hardest. The reason the design phase feels so cut and dry is because it is so final. It's your one shot at delivering the feelings you want your customers to have when they enter your storefront. You probably won't be messing with the design much after this point, so it does take some thought before you launch into the process.

In the last chapter, I got you started planning your site and thinking about your blog layout. You've already taken some time to sketch out your blog template layout, navigation menus, blog topics, and considered a color scheme. These are major first steps toward designing an organized blog and is going to prove a wonderful foundation for the actual designing phase which we're going to launch into now. So if you've already taken notes from the last chapter, then you're ready to move forward!

Hire a designer or do it yourself?

First things first: you'll need to consider if you'd like to hire out your design or tackle it yourself. There are definitely some pros and cons to either.

DIY Pros:

- Anytime you do something yourself, you usually save money.
- You have more control over the creation of your graphics and can edit them anytime you wish.
- You won't need to explain your vision to a designer in hopes that your final product results in what you envisioned.
- Lower risk financially and time-wise. Your turnaround time invested will be as slow or quick as you like. You're in charge.

DIY Cons:

- If you consider yourself graphically impaired, the challenge of pairing up the right colors and creating images might be overwhelming.
- If your final design elements look unprofessional, so will your business.
- The time you spend attempting to figure out a graphics program may feel like a wasted investment if you could simply hire it out to a professional.

Really, mompreneurs, the choice is totally and completely yours. Whether you decide to design your own blog or hire someone to design for you is a choice that you have to make personally. Only you know what is best for your business.

I'm going to explain some things you should look for in choosing to hire a designer. Then if you're still determined to do it yourself, I'll teach you how to set up your own blog and design a header and graphics.

And just so you know, I have been on both sides of the coin. I love working with, creating, and manipulating my own graphics. I've also hired professional designers for some of my projects. From that perspective, I can give you a unique outlook on what to look for no matter which boat you find yourself in.

How to hire a designer

If you've chosen to be completely hands-off with your blog design, I understand! And if this is the best decision for your business, congrats for coming to this conclusion. It takes courage to admit when you're simply not good at something and need to hire it out. It's better to accept this fact up front rather than spending precious time working on something you don't enjoy. If you don't enjoy designing, then there are plenty of designers who would love to help you.

There are a few things you should look out for when hiring a designer, however. I wouldn't recommend doing a google search for "web designer" because you'll end up with a barrage of choices, many of which may not be the best fit for you.

Find a designer who is in your niche.

One of my first designers had a knack for helping women in business and authors with their graphic design needs. I was attracted to her because of her specialty, and I felt that she would understand my needs better than a designer who didn't know much about my niche. I was correct. Her feminine touch and her understanding of my niche market allowed her creative freedom in designing the perfect banner for my blog in 2010.

Ask yourself: "Am I this designer's target market?" If you are, then you may be the perfect client for them, and you may have found your match.

Study their design portfolio.

This goes without saying. If you don't look at the work they've previously done, how will you know they can give you what you want? Look at their work samples and discover some of their most recent projects.

Who have they designed for? What is their design style like? Do their designs resonate with you? Would you like a design similar to one of their recent projects?

Read client testimonials.

Testimonials can be a tell-all, but only if you get personal. Of course, a designer is only going to publish the best testimonials on their blog. Read this, of course. After you read them, visit the blogs which they designed to get a feel for how the blog pulled together. And if you want to dig deeper and a get a personal opinion of their work, contact one of their clients and ask for a personal recommendation.

Find out their fees.

You're almost done with your homework in the hire-a-designer department. You may want to reserve this step for last, or do it first thing- depending on your preference. My experience is that oftentimes we rule out a potential working relationship with an awesome designer based on design fees listed on their site that scare us away! Don't let pricing scare you, even if it may appear to be above industry-standard. First do your research (as outlined above), and if you truly believe the designer may be a good fit for you, reach out to them and ask for a payment plan. Ask if there are discounts and specials available and when. (Some designers run seasonal specials during holidays.)

The fact is: you need a blog and a creative design that expresses your business accurately. You want to be proud of your design: your storefront. So think of this as a long-term investment.

The end result will hopefully be one of satisfaction with your final product.

Questions to ask your designer

While your designer will be asking YOU questions to prepare for the design process, here are a few questions you may want to ask the designer:

- How much do you charge and can you please explain your fee structure? (What is your basic design package, and what are considered "extras"?)
- What was your most favorite project, and why was it your favorite?
- What software applications will you be using to design my site?
- What questions do you have for me before beginning this project?

Having a good line of communication open between you and your designer will prove critical in the process. You'll be more likely to get what you want out of the deal and end up with a blog design you can be proud of.

A DIY Design Plan

So, for the rest of you do-it-yourselfers, I have something for you, too!

Not everyone is willing to shell out the big bucks to commit to a blog design. Believe me, I get that, and I completely understand. Though I have to err on the side of caution when encouraging you to design your own blog (especially if you are NOT a designer), there are definitely exceptions to the rule.

You may feel that it isn't financially feasible for you to invest a few dollars toward a blog design at the beginning stage of your business startup, and that's completely understandable. Most solopreneurs are not swimming in startup cash, and as a mom, wife, friend, or community volunteer, you probably have your money tied up in many different directions. Although it's not imperative that you hire a professional, I highly encourage you to save back some cash to invest in this one bit of your business: your virtual storefront.

However, if now is just not the right time to hire a designer and you're committed to doing it yourself, allow me to show you a few steps toward making this blog design come together with the least amount of stress possible. I have been designing my own headers and graphics for years and understand the importance of learning to do these things for myself in the case that a designer is not around to help me.

Let's start with setting up your blog.

Installing WordPress

My current blogging platform of choice is WordPress. At the moment of my writing this, I feel that WordPress (the open source version found at Worpress.org) is the strongest and most versatile blogging platform available for today's web entrepreneur.

Before you can install WordPress, you'll actually need to back up just a minute and grab yourself some online space. You have your domain name already, and I gave an example earlier using GoDaddy as your domain name provider. GoDaddy is great for other services as well. Your domain name gives your blog the title. (Think: your virtual store name on display at the entrance.) It's separate from your hosting (which I'll discuss next), but can be purchased along with hosting- just to make things easier.

So your next step is to set up the other service you'll need: **hosting.** Use any hosting provider you wish. Among these providers are some of the bigger names like Bluehost, Hostgator, GoDaddy, and SiteGround. Hosting gives you the storage you need for your blog. It's your blog's home.

If you're a newbie at this and you're determined to be a DIY-er (a true do-it-yourself gal), then I would suggest the easier route of purchasing both your domain name and hosting at one company . Purchasing them from separate companies makes set up just a tad trickier, but it can be done. I personally host my sites with SiteGround but in the past when I hosted with another company I had to take a few extra steps to connect my hosting and domain. So my recommendation would be, if you're just starting out, to simply buy it all in-house if possible. And again, companies such as Bluehost or SiteGround does it all.

So, you have your domain name and hosting. You now have a website. Well...sort of. You haven't begun developing the site yet, so in the public eye- when your domain name is typed in, what they see is a "parked" page, or maybe even an error message. So we have a bit more work to do.

You ready for the fun part? Alright, DIY-ers! Roll up your sleeves and get ready to design.

Working it with WordPress!

There are tons of web development systems out there. Back in the late 90's I designed all my sites using HTML and learned some markup language and cascading style sheets. Eventually, I progressed from Microsoft FrontPage to Macromedia Dreamweaver. Don't know what I'm referring to? That's okay because it's erring on the side of old school site design talk. Today it's all about WordPress. Other valuable blog/site design services are also coming to the forefront.

Designing on WordPress, for me, is easier, it's more efficient, and it's content on steroids. The RSS feed (you know that ability to subscribe to content on a blog or subscribe to a podcast?) is what makes WordPress such a viable life source for your online business.

If you're on the fence about which blogging platform to use, think no further. Selecting WordPress will pay off in the end and will make your online business easier for you.

And if you're unsure about whether you should invest in the self-hosted WordPress.org or use the free version (WordPress.com), think no further. If you've already gone the length of purchasing a hosting company and domain name, you've already begun your branding process, and will therefore need to self-host your WordPress through Wordpress.org (available as a quick install on most hosting control panels). You will appreciate this decision as you find out just how much designing flexibility and variety of plugin options are available to enhance your business.

Next steps for setup? Check with your hosting company to find out how to install WordPress. In many hosting companies (GoDaddy, Hostgator, and Bluehost), installing WordPress is a one-click option. Easy peasy. Once it's installed, you now have access to a powerful engine. It's your hangout behind-the-scenes to keep things rolling smoothly for the storefront.

Now log into your WordPress dashboard. It should look something like this:

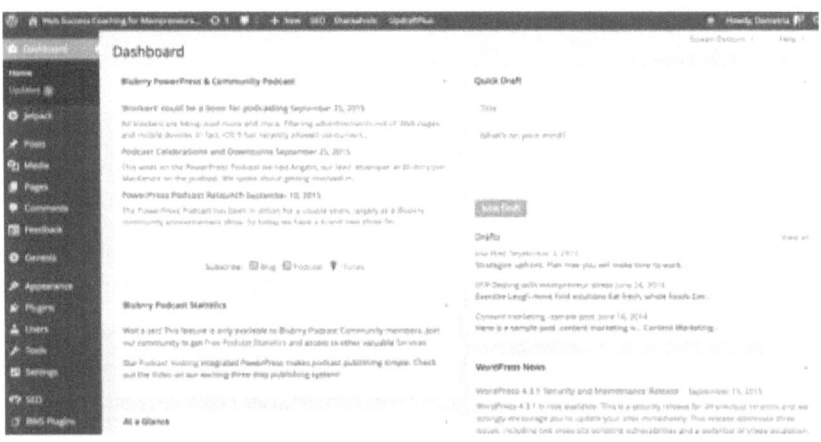

If you're new to WordPress, familiarize yourself with the dashboard- where you'll write posts, install plugins, change settings, add media, and switch themes. And speaking of themes, here's another area where I am very opinionated when it comes to the design process.

There are so many free themes available, many of which look pretty decent. But as a business owner, I should probably caution you against installing free themes on your site for several reasons:

a. **Free themes can be unstable.** So, if something goes wrong with the theme (the code inadvertently breaks after you install a plugin, for example), you're out of luck- and your online business loses sales for the duration of the time you need to spend re-designing with a new theme.

b. **Free themes are typically unsupported.** No help desk to call or support tickets to submit when you're in a fix with your theme equals trouble for you and your business.

So, those are my two main reasons for not using free themes.

Meanwhile, one search engine inquiry for paid themes to use for your site will turn up a multitude of options and you will be exhausted just looking at the options. So...here's where I help!

The good news is, I have two main theme recommendations that are used widely in the professional blogging world- one of which I have used consistently for the past half decade and have nothing but good to say about.

The first is Woo themes. I haven't used it at all but know many professional bloggers who do and who swear by it. They have a nice theme selection and are "supported by real people", according to their website- which is a real plus for any support you might need during the process.

The second is Genesis themes, which I have been using since 2010. Many of my sites run on Genesis by StudioPress and I find that it has been easy for me to get my questions answered and help with coding issues during the development process. Their message boards just for members is really helpful, as well as the documentation supporting each theme that guides me through the setup process. Additionally, StudioPress widgets make website building an exciting adventure! I've also recently discovered Divi, a drag and drop design platform which makes designing easier for newbies.

At any rate, find a well-supported theme to purchase, and then get to know your theme inside and out. If you're planning to do this yourself rather than hire out, you'll need to become very familiar with how to create navigation menus, install and set up plugins, setting up widgets and controlling spam (very important!)

Plugin recommendations

If my blog were a human body, plugins would be like the nerves- sending impulses throughout my blog. Plugins are such a crucial part of how I run my blogging business that without them my blog would be rather drab and almost lifeless.

Here are my specific plugin recommendations based on ten years of a combination of playing around with and seriously using different ones until I found my favorites!

You should definitely consider installing:

- Google Analytics (set that up in Google first under your account)
- Spam control plugins like Akismet
- Contact forms (choose from any variety in the search plugins section)
- Any social media plugins (like Comment Luv, Shareaholic, Pinterest Pin It, and Jetpack)
- An author bio plugin like WP Biographia.
- One way to design behind the scenes until you're

ready for the big website reveal is to install the Under Construction plugin which allows you to toggle on/off so when you're done designing you can turn it off and do your quick launch reveal
- I also highly recommend you find a plugin which allows you to back up your data on a scheduled basis in case something goes wrong (you just never know). I currently use UpdraftPlus. Find one that works for you and get it installed and working quickly.
- One last plugin to arm your site with is the highly-recommended Yoast SEO. This plugin allows you to think about your search engine optimization with each blog post without the need to become an expert.

Be careful not to overdo it on the plugins, though, or it can slow your site down, unfortunately.

I know this is a lot, but if you ever find yourself needing specific help with any of this, there is always the option to hire out this part of the project. You can also just send me a note and set up a coaching appointment with me where I'll walk you through the steps pertinent to your particular situation.

But at this point- if you've gotten this far- you deserve huge congrats! You have made major strides toward setting up the engine on which your business will run.

But one thing I didn't mention yet was the actual design. Ahh...let's not forget the fun part! For those of you who love the imagery and visual aspect of your project- and if you're just designers at heart, then this part should be fun.

Designing your blog

Your blog design really all depends on your theme and

setup. If you're a real pro at WordPress theme developing and designing, then skip this part of the book and just go for it! Do what you do and make your blog design fabulous!

However, many of us are not actually design pros, and some of us know very little about how to make a blog look even remotely decent. If you're still determined to dig your heels in and make a go of doing this yourself, I highly recommend you really observe some blogs whose designs you admire. Think about what it is you like about their design and layout, color schemes, symmetry, graphics. If you feel you can do this, then I have a few tips for you to help make the process easier.

If at this point, however, you realize that designing is not your strength, then be a big girl and hire someone who actually loves to design and can give you the fabulous look you visualize! I truly mean this in the kindest way possible. It takes a big person to admit when she's not the best at something. In fact, it's women who realize their weaknesses and know when to build their network that actually succeed quickly in their businesses.

But for those of you DIY-ers (like myself) that keep forging ahead to try it on your own, here are a few tips that might actually help you save money and create something you're proud of:

1. Check your template's documentation for the **suggested dimensions for your site header.** Keep these dimensions in mind because you'll need this when designing your logo.
2. **Design your logo.** I use Adobe Photoshop (available at around $20 per month for the entire Adobe suite). You can also use PicMonkey or Canva which is free. Create a new image using the suggested dimensions. Be sure to pick a color palette which

will be a consistent theme throughout the entire site. Your logo will usually set the tone for the blog and for your business, so choose carefully. If you're feeling unsure about this, please hire it out. Fiverr might be an option, but I have had much better success hiring a graphic designer who knew and understood my needs (and the money I paid her was worth it). I also create the majority of my logos today after many years of creating in Photoshop, but only after years of experience have I developed a comfort zone in that area. Your logo or site header is the one thing you want to make sure you really have right- so I don't recommend you cut corners here. But again, if you feel confident, go for it.

3. **Tweak your theme colors to match your logo.** Okay, this is going to require some careful stepping around in the coding documentation. If you're comfortable with cascading style sheets (the set of rules which basically tells your blog which colors and fonts to display as well as other design behaviors), then you'll appreciate the liberty you have to change your colors and fonts and such. For this tweaking, you'll need to find your "appearance" tab in the dashboard and click "editor". There you will find your stylesheet (under "style.css"). From here you can change nearly anything: from the colors and fonts of your navigation menus, title displays, headings, footers, and more. To change colors you'll need to be familiar with how to change color hex codes (color pickers in Adobe Photoshop or Illustrator help.)

Here are a few more design tips to keep in mind:

1. **Remember that simple is best.** Don't go overboard with colors. Use white backgrounds when possible

rather than patterns. Stick with a simple color palette of no more than 3-4 colors.
2. **Keep your navigation uncluttered.** Be sure to make your site navigation as simplified as possible. Your navigation should be uncluttered and make sense to the reader. Place your most pertinent information on the main navigation bar and take advantage of the drop menu feature to categorize a submenu if needed.
3. **Make your home page define your purpose.** It's always a good idea for site visitors to understand what your business offers in one fell swoop. Be sure your homepage is distinguished as an entrance page to invite your readers to read more. But first, they need a nice introduction to what you do. Try to clarify this with a header that defines who you are and what you do with your personal picture or logo and tagline and motto. This works especially well for service-based businesses. If you sell products, a nice photo of your product on the front page can do the trick.
4. **Set up your mailing list.** As part of your web development process, don't forget to include the plugins or codes that allow your website to engage your audience. I'll talk more about engagement later on in the book, but for now, if you already have your mailing list provider service set up (which you will absolutely need to do before you open shop), go ahead and grab that special code they give you and copy and paste it (either into a widget or home page- but check your documentation first.)

Whew! Okay, so that was a LOT of work. Yes- it's work. But we mompreneurs don't shy away from the work it takes to set up and run a successful business. And remember, you don't have to do all the work yourself. Hire some of these things out if you need to.

For me, I personally get a kick out of designing my own blogs- but that's because I like to dig into the coding, take things apart, and put them back together. Basically, I love hacking my sites apart so I can figure out how it works and then rebuilding it from scratch. But that's just me, and I absolutely don't expect everyone to have that geek love for code or design.

So don't get bogged down with coding and designing and find yourself giving up on your blogging goals altogether because you're stuck figuring out how to tweak your theme. Hire the help you need and keep moving forward.

So now, your site is designed. You're ready to push "publish". Or are you? What next?

Chapter 6: Position yourself as an expert.

I often tell women in business that beyond all the technical jargon and the hard work of pulling together the actual website (domain name, hosting, designing and developing the blog), there is the even greater work of establishing your expertise.

You, my friend, are an amazing expert! Set yourself up that way and you're on your way to blogging success.

Let's talk for a minute about positioning.

When people visit your blog, first impressions are everything. Ask a friend or colleague to take a look at your blog and give you some constructive criticism. (I do it all the time and my husband is completely honest but helpful!)

Ask your friendly critics if they understand what your blog is about. Do they understand at first glance what products and services you offer? Do you stand out as an expert in your industry? How can you improve?

Okay, let's deal really quickly with that little nagging issue many women deal with: the issue of FEAR. I dealt with it earlier in this book, but let's recap:

Fear is False Evidence Appearing Real. (That acronym helps me remember why I don't need to fear.)

What that means is, if you've been taught growing up that you should stay "humble", stay quiet, don't talk about yourself- then you'll need to do some major rewiring of the way you think about business. You can easily develop a fear of success by falling into the trap of false humility.

If you're afraid to stand out, then you won't. If you're afraid to lead, then you simply won't.

But if you step out in faith (the opposite of fear, by the way), you'll give yourself the freedom to set yourself up as an expert.

The problem is, many women are waiting for someone else to tell you whether you are an expert or not. But the key is knowing who you are. You don't have to be rolling in millions or have landed several television appearances and radio interviews before you can consider yourself an expert. Free yourself to believe in yourself.

You are an expert because you have experience. You are an expert because you have passion. You are an expert because you have knowledge to pass on to someone else. You are an expert because you have a product that is a solution to someone's problem.

The amount of money, web traffic, or notoriety you have today does not affect your expertise. You can be an expert without those things. But you'll need those things in order for your expertise to eventually bring the income you want.

So, we've established your expertise. You **are** an expert. Now, we can move on to developing your purpose, vision, and brand through your blog.

LET'S TALK ABOUT PURPOSE.

Target market, brand identity, and voice are all key concepts that will be important points of discussion later on in this book. But in order to bring these concepts to fruition, you must first churn your newly found passion into a clearly defined purpose for your business. Your business purpose then will make room for your overall vision. I'll explain how this works.

Let's first start with the cornerstone of your business: your purpose. Before you begin any project, you always have a goal. That overall goal is essentially your purpose. You can have more than one goal, but your purpose remains steadfast and is the epitome of all your business goals. Here's what I mean:

Let's say your business goals are:

1. to **teach** solopreneurs how to self-publish,
2. give business owners the **tools** for self-publishing
3. and provide an opportunity for authors to **use your publishing company** to get their book published and promoted.

(You can also have goals related to the amount of money you wish to make, the growth of your company over the years, and more.)

In this example, you have several business goals: teaching, providing tools (advice, support, software), and offering publishing services. In just one sentence, how would you sum it all up into one overall goal?

You could say that your goal is to provide training, resources, and services to teach and promote the works of self-published authors. Of course, there are a variety of ways to word it, but this is just one example. Using your overall business goal, this summary will help you to simplify the direction for your business. Essentially, you now have a business purpose that you can focus on. And remember, what you focus on expands.

Your VISION

Now that you have a few goals written down, let's talk about your company vision. A vision helps you to clarify what you want your company to achieve in a broad sense over a period of time. A vision affects how your values and core beliefs affect your company in the long run. Without short-term and long-term vision, your company doesn't have enough sustaining power to make it through the tough times. Take some time to consider your business vision and you'll breathe life into your business blog. Essentially, your vision will help to answer the following questions:

- How will your business have grown one year/five years/ten years from now?
- Will you have changed locations? (a new office maybe?)
- Revenue and cash flow: how will it have changed over the years?
- Will you hire employees or virtual assistants, and how will this change your business processes?
- How will your passion for this business be sustained over the years?
- How many hours a day, week, or month will you work?

Since your vision and your goals go hand in hand, we'll make this one complete activity. Take a few moments to complete your vision and goal-planning in your notebook.

Planning your blog like you would a business is essential if you plan to see a consistent and steady income. It all begins with your passion and follows up with your purpose and vision. So let's go ahead and get these squared away before we move on.

Defining your Unique Selling Point

Some call this your unique selling proposition, or your USP. In business, this simply means that you choose to differentiate your service in order to engage the clients and customers that you truly want to attract. In order to define your business clearly, you must know the key elements that set you apart from the crowd.

There are obviously other business owners in your niche. There are a lot of other bloggers who blog about the same thing you do and who may offer very similar products or services. Having and knowing your USP is the one trick to having a leg up in your industry.

You will always have "competitors". (I say this rather tongue-in-cheek since I don't like to use the word much.)

Take advantage of this by researching your competition thoroughly, figuring out what their strengths and weaknesses are. Then make a list of what your own business strengths and weaknesses are.

Take an overall comparison of these two lists and make a clear distinction between yourself and your competitors. What do they offer that you don't? What do they offer that you would not want to offer? What do they not offer they you do? How do they sell their products and how would you sell differently? In other words, ask questions that lead you to discover what differentiates you from those in your niche market.

Discovering your customer avatar

We also really need to look at your target market and ask yourself what your followers really want and need. Considering your customer avatar is a very important part of running a successful business. Who is your target market and why? Who do you really set out to serve and what solutions do you bring to their problems?

The biggest of these questions is how do you solve your customer's problems? In order to have an answer for this question, you need to know what their problems are. Take some time to write down a list of at least 5 problems your prospects have and how your business can solve them.

I've taken time to do this exercise. Here are my answers:

My customer avatar is a woman (and more specifically, a mom) with passion and purpose who just needs the proper tools, resources, and guidance to make her online business a success. More specifically, she may have any of the following attributes:

1. Has the desire to begin an online business, but needs guidance
2. Has an online business, but needs a success strategy
3. Wants to create digital products but lacks the skill or motivation
4. Wants to build a lucrative business, but has trouble balancing business with family life
5. Feels overwhelmed with getting her business off the ground and needs a support system in place

A general view of my customer avatar is as follows. She is:

1. female
2. between the age range of 25-55
3. very likely to have children
4. is very active in her children's lives
5. has likely earned a college degree
6. may currently work in a career she is ready to leave
7. works flexibly as an entrepreneur
8. may be a stay at home mom
9. would describe herself as goal-driven
10. wants to increase/leverage her income while raising a family
11. her main concern is maintaining close family connections while running her business
12. cares about family values while balancing a business
13. she also cares about maintaining a holistic approach to life and business
14. her biggest fears: she will grow her business too large, or that she will fail at business
15. she also fears neglecting her most important priorities in life: family and friends
16. she is likely a spiritual person
17. she dreams of owning a business that syncs with her values
18. she buys my products and services to help her overcome business fears
19. she buys my products to give her practical instructions to creating her business blog
20. she likes to read motivational books, parenting magazines, business books
21. she is probably a product junkie
22. she listens to business podcasts
23. she is subscribed to both business and parenting video channels on YouTube or Vimeo
24. she attends virtual business workshops, and loves inspirational radio stations
25. she infuses her life with positivity

26. she most values her own integrity and her relationships with those closest to her
27. she is careful about how she approaches business.

Now, see if you can come up with at least five personality traits for your customer avatar. (I've given you 27!)

Decide which problems they have that you know you can solve.

Voice and Branding

Now that you know what sets you apart from the crowd, let's talk about clarifying your voice. You want to make sure that who you are as an individual- in other words, your personality- is interwoven throughout your business blog.

Believe me, you can be both personal and professional, and your audience will love you for it. The bottom line is: just be yourself. I'm going to show you how to do that.

We've spoken about determining your purpose, clarifying your vision, and differentiating your business from your competitors. The next best thing you can do for yourself is to establish your voice, making it resoundingly clear who your target audience is and connecting with your readers, listeners, and viewers in an engaging and personal way.

Your message is the key to your business. Your USP helps to distinguish you from other businesses like yours, but it's your underlying core message- your business purpose- that should be the overall tone for everything you do in your business. If your purpose is to teach dog owners how to train puppies, then keep this goal in mind in every aspect of your business. Your goal should influence the way in which you interact with your prospects. I'll show you what I mean by that.

There are two elements to defining your business voice that I like to focus on. I call them **infusion and engagement.**

Infusion (infusing your personality throughout your content) through:

- word choice
- style
- tone

Infusion is the art of allowing your personality to permeate throughout your content in such a way that your voice becomes distinct from all others in your niche. Your readers will know your voice and connect with your message because it comes from you. That true connection comes from an infusion of your personality throughout your entire business presence. What this means is that your choice of words, your style, and your tone all make a difference in your presentation.

For example, if you pepper your blog posts with exciting, action-filled words, if your tone motivates and your style is professional, knee-jerk, or friendly, you will better be able to make the right types of connections with your audience and even attract the best prospects to your message. The tribe that you want on board with you will come aboard because they resonate with not only your message but also your personality.

This leads me to the second facet of true connection with your audience: **engagement.**

There are three ways in particular in which we engage with our customers and clients:

1. personal connections (email/direct messages)
2. social media (broadcast messages),
3. and our content (blogs, videos, podcasts, newsletters)

Your personality shines through your business through your **content.** Your content consists of your blog activity and your mailing list, as well as videos or podcasts and other forms of media in which you share your message.

Any time you write a blog post or send out a newsletter you are connecting with your readers by sharing your thoughts and opinions. Your readers can then respond to your newsletter with a reply or grace your blog with a comment. This type of engagement is invaluable for all involved. You want to make the most of your blog content, being sure to give the cream of the crop of your ideas and put your best foot forward. Your content is being judged by the quality of your offerings, your opinions and how you express them, and the solutions you bring to your readers. Your reader wants the best of you, so make sure you give them your very best. Content may come in the form of blog posts, newsletters, podcasts, videos, and workshops.

You can also shine through **social media.** Your personality is exuded through each tweet, update, pin, or share. If your business personality is serious, outgoing, or upbeat, you can definitely create a social media strategy that matches your mood. Social media should work alongside your content to create a systematic process of getting your message across to your prospects.

Again, it's your underlying core message (i.e-teaching dog owners about puppy training) that will be the focus of all of your content and social media strategies. When you learn to relax into your online personality, creating a virtual world in which you can share your thoughts freely, your platform will speak volumes to your readers, viewers, and listeners. Using your God-given personality will take your business to the next level; and as an online visionary or solopreneur, it is truly the only way to create that successful business online!

The last leg of engagement is the personal connection- through **direct messages or email.** For this, you'll need two things: a.) active social media accounts and b.) a mailing list. You will use your social media accounts (twitter, for example) to connect personally with prospects or potential jv (joint venture) partners through direct message. I've found it to be particularly useful during my down times to open up my twitter account and shoot over a quick greeting to someone I'd like to interview or partner with in some fashion.

Direct messaging is key to personal communication online. Your tribe already loves your content. They follow your blog, watch your videos, listen to your podcast, read your newsletter. Now, it's time to reach out and personally engage with them. From time to time, visit your mailing list and shoot a quick email to one of your subscribers asking for feedback. Look up one of your followers on twitter and engage in personal conversation with them. Say hello to or mention a Facebook fan. You can find fun and creative ways to connect with your followers personally. One way I enjoyed engaging at one of my blogs was through giveaways. Our readers feel special, even **loved**, when they participate in and even win a contest!

BRANDING

Branding is essentially creating a name, design, or idea for your company that identifies your business and differentiates you from other products or services. Your voice, your tone, your chosen forms of social media, how you relate to your customers, your logo- is all part of your established branding.

By this point, you have already had your blog designed and logo created and are already on the path to establishing your visual brand. Be sure to place your logo everywhere. Many solopreneurs choose to use taglines at the end of email messages that help to establish your identity. For example, at the end of each of my podcasts and blog posts, I like to add the tag: "To Your Web Success". This little endeavor allows my listeners and readers to understand that my goal at [Mompreneurs In Heels](#) is to help you find success in your own personal entrepreneurial journey. I'm like your virtual cheerleader and business friend toasting your success because I believe in you already.

As mentioned previously, your voice is important and is also part of your branding. Make sure you stick to the tone that most closely portrays the message you want to give. Ritzy, conversational, warm and bubbly, or knee-jerk- it's completely up to you.

Let's take a moment here and discuss some ideas about using your voice and tone in business. If you are having trouble understanding this concept, just think of the way you normally speak to your friends and family. How do you sound? Are you anxious, relaxed, excited, or intense? What is your personality like?

Remember, in business - and especially as a solopreneur- you want to sound as natural as possible. If you are not naturally energetic, then your more laid-back approach may be the key to setting a tone for your business that you will be comfortable with in the long run.

I'll give you an example of two sales pitches with opposite tones. Think about which one you most resonate with:

Sales Pitch 1:

"Dog owners, you HAVE to understand that offering your puppy organic food is By FAR the BEST choice you can make for your dog and for your family. The additives and GMOs in non-organic dog food are making our dogs SICK and you would be absolutely nuts to keep feeding your dog garbage. Believe me when I say your dog will thank you a million times over by simply making a switch to organic dog food like the brand my company offers: Dogz Organics. Today I'm offering a BOGO sale. Buy any one can of puppy chow and get one free. I'll also throw in an extra organic oatmeal dog biscuit, plus a 10% off coupon, but you have to act NOW!"

Or... Sales Pitch 2:

"I truly believe in what we do at Dogz Organics, and everything we offer in our store are GMO-free, pesticide-free, and organic, as well as specifically crafted for your dog. The environment we live in isn't the healthiest, but our dogs can be healthy. I know you care about your dog and want the best for your furry friend. Offering the cleanest products and high grade dog foods is a decision that will both positively affect your dog and your environment. With a healthier dog on your hands you have less worries for your pooch as you'll lower the chances of illnesses and infections simply by switching to a better quality dog food. Our boutique offers a variety of healthy options for your dog. Please come by for a visit at on our online boutique and email me directly if you have any questions at all. During my online office hours of 2-5 p.m. I am available for consulting and can offer you a 10% discount on any purchase, plus a free gift after your first purchase of $20.00 or more. I truly look forward to hearing from you...and your dog!"

Which tone is more like yours? Again, these were very extreme examples, but they help get my point across.

The cut-throat, buy-it-now approach actually works for many people because it resonates with those who need the action-inspired, provocative kick in the pants. It's not my preferred approach because I don't respond to it. I prefer the second, and if you are more laid-back you may find the second pitch an easier one to handle in your own business.

Which of these pitches would receive instant action? It all depends. It depends on the kinds of people you are trying to reach, and their personalities. It depends on what your mailing list subscribers respond well to.

We can't always determine their responses, but we can determine the tone that we are more comfortable carrying in our business. The tone you choose needs to fit you like a glove so that you can sound natural. Your sales pitch needs to sound like you, and not like anyone else. So be yourself.

Another tip to remember is: branding also consists of being consistent! Try to use the same color scheme, logos, visuals, and taglines throughout your social media channels and blog.

Addressing the Needs of Your Prospects

Research your target market's needs effectively is an important aspect of your business that you cannot neglect. You've already uncovered your customer avatar, but now we need to dig a little deeper and figure out exactly how to address their needs.

Once you have a clear picture and running list of your target market, your customer's avatar, and his or her specific needs, you can move forward on preparing how you will address those needs. So go ahead and pull out your customer avatar notes and review them. What are the most pressing needs? Go ahead and begin thinking of a plan to address those specific needs. This will, of course, need to be addressed in the form of your products and your services.

Which products will you offer that will help your customer? Which services will you offer? How can you improve upon the products and services you already offer?

Start a new page, listing services and products you will

create or offer in the next month, 6 months, and year. Develop them and update your prospects periodically on the progress, letting them know that you took into account their needs and that you are creating this product or service just for them.

Which services do you currently offer that you can improve upon? How do your current services currently fail to address your customer's needs? Use this as a starting point.

For example, if your online organic dog treats boutique offers products only, but you oftentimes receive many emails from your customers with questions about dog care, take that as a sign that you could possibly add consulting to your business repertoire.

Or if your customers are asking for more products for grooming but you only offer food and treats, you might want to consider adding grooming items. Really listen to your customer and address their needs.

Another thing to consider is focusing on connection strategies that work. How do your customers prefer to be contacted? Produce a survey and ask for their opinions. I recently did this and discovered that 98% of my newsletter subscribers appreciate reading my newsletters and listening to my podcasts first, then watching my videos second, and attending webinars last. And it makes sense. I have a group of busy women who have their own businesses and families to take care of- and sitting down to watch a video is oftentimes out of the question for many of them- at least for those who are on the go and just want info quick.

It's one of my personal business goals to create content that can be devoured in different ways. So while I offer video, I like to also offer audio and quick show notes in my blog posts for those interested in the audio version.

And then there are those who just like to visit my blog and skim the posts for updates- so I need to make sure my content is there, too. For those who are ready to bite the bullet and want to work with me in a coaching session, they can have the full version of what I offer.

Think about the different connection strategies you can use to make sure you are meeting all the needs of your clients and customers.

The Expertise Setup

So how do experts truly become good at selling their expertise? Glad you asked.

Well, besides winning the hearts of your "tribe" (your community), you need to have a workable system in place that allows you to revolve your blog around your product or service.

If you're selling homemade dog biscuits, be sure your blog posts show your knowledge on dog treats. With every blog post lead your reader back to a product link where they can purchase, but only after you've provided them quality content.

If you're selling your expertise as a personal stylist, then blog regularly about fashion, and be sure to include links to your consultation sign-up page in each blog post. Always leave your readers with a takeaway. Offer freebies or discounts once in a while. Conduct contests and give away free consults to the lucky blog winner.

The idea here is to allow your product or service be the core of your blog. (Remember those keywords we gathered earlier? Now's the time to use them on each blog post!)

You want to center your free content (blog posts, newsletters, free audios and videos) around the core product and service that you are selling.

If you're a service-based business, another important fact to remember is not giving away more than you should. Your time is a precious commodity, so my recommendation is not to book yourself rock solid for months on end because of your ongoing free 30-minute consult offer. (Remember, you need time for actual paying clients.) Maybe place a time limit on how long you will give away your free consult time, or consider offering a free digital product instead.

Of course, my advice changes if you're not a solopreneur and actually have a team backing you up. Then by all means, if your free consults give you the quality leads you're looking for and you have the time to keep up, keep doing what you're doing.

COLLECTING PAYMENT

By now, you've already decided on your main products or services to sell and you've set up your blog as a virtual store, ready to reach your target market and bring in your customers. Now it's time to get paid.

If you're selling products, you should consider an e-commerce WordPress plugin like WPeCommerce or WooCommerce. Better yet, you could simply rely on good ol' Paypal. These plugins are easy to set up, as is Paypal. Looking into Stripe may be worthwhile also. Setting up your payment collection is a very important step in getting paid online.

Chapter 7: Develop the perfect blogging routine.

You've come so far, mompreneur! You've set up shop and now you're ready to begin working your business through the power of your blog. Go ahead and take out your notebook and consider what topics you'll want to discuss on your blog.

Finding what to blog about

Figuring out what to talk about may seem like a daunting task at first, but don't let it stump you. Finding topics for your blog is really much easier than you might think. It's all about staying open to the world around you and gathering the sometimes more-obvious-than-usual clues.

You can use the keywords you gathered earlier to help you find blog topics, and I always recommend you do that as well. But you'll also want to think of your customer avatar and what her greatest needs are.

You'll want to be sure to write posts to address the questions of your potential clients, your target market- and not just think about developing posts around your central keyword theme. A combination of both of these methods is the best way to develop a meaningful blog. In other words, a handful of good keywords plus the knowledge of what your audience is talking about can help you maintain the best balance for blog topic ideas.

There are several ways to come up with good post ideas. You could perform a reverse engineering search in Google by typing in a question you feel your target market might be asking. From here, locate the website which answers the question and comb through that page for additional questions that might have been asked about the same topic.

Another idea is to subscribe to blogs in your niche. Find blog posts which solve problems or answers questions and derive some of your own topics from those ideas. Don't forget to read the comments section of their posts and see what readers are saying and asking. There are oftentimes hidden topic idea goldmines in the comments section of blog posts.

Search message boards in your niche and find out what people are asking. Message boards are not the thing these days, but they still exist and you can mine them for valuable data. Visit YouTube channels and Google Plus pages or join Facebook groups and read conversations. Don't forget about Pinterest. I get a ton of writing ideas just by taking a few minutes out of my week to pin to my idea boards. Getting on social media is an excellent way to determine the problems of your target market and the solutions that are already available for them.

Once you've found your topics, now it's time to set up a blogging routine.

Setting up your blogging routine.

You're a busy mom, a daughter, perhaps a wife, a friend, a confidant, a colleague, and maybe even a chauffeur, tutor, and counselor (which mom isn't?), and life gets busy. Simple as that.

So, besides the idea of running your business, when will you have time to blog?

That's a good question.

This is why it's so important to think of your blog as an integral part of your business. In fact, it's the heart and soul of your online business. And if you own a brick and mortar too, then your blog should be a major player in your sales. Or at least that's what we want.

So, back to the burning question: *how do you find time to blog?*

Well, to answer that question quite frankly, I'd have to ask you to remember how important your blog is to your business. Once you've established that your blog is a huge priority in the way your business is set up and that without your blog your business either crumbles or doesn't have much traction, then you will understand the power of setting aside time to blog.

Now, that doesn't mean you need to blog 5 times per week, but it is important to keep a goal in mind to have regular communication via your blog with your readers.

Just a side note: I used to be gung-ho about updating my blogs, at minimum 3-5 times per week. I did this for years on one blog while updating my other two at least once a week. Eventually, life caught up with me, and after several moves and illnesses, I realized that my blogging schedule would have to be placed on hold in order to deal with life. My advice to you is to create a routine that works for you, but give yourself the flexibility to call on a break when you need one.

In general, a brand new blog needs to gain traction in the marketplace (we're thinking Google search here). In order for Google to find you, you need to be visible there. And in order to be visible, you need to have content

Have you heard the phrase "content is king"? There is a reason that saying resonates with so many marketers. Think of your blog as a business enterprise. The more you add to your business, the bigger and stronger it becomes. You can also think of your blog as a book. The more content you add, the more pages you accrue. The more pages you have, the bigger your book becomes. You want your blog to eventually become a very, very thick manual with pages in Google's archives for years to come. In this way, you will become a noted subject expert surrounding your blog's central theme.

Remember the anchor keywords I asked you to decide on earlier? If you use your keywords smartly throughout each "page" or post of your blog, you'll soon become a subject expert for that keyword. No promises here, but this could eventually open the door for business opportunities and partnerships. It will also help those looking for your content to find you. It's exactly what happened for me. For years I ranked pretty high for certain keywords pertaining to homeschooling (I used a handful of them throughout my blog). Within months of applying the keyword strategy, I began to watch my homeschooling blog, ChristianHomeschoolMoms.com, rise to the second and then the first results page in Google. As a result, when companies would search for information on homeschool moms, my site would pop up on the first results page. I have been contacted over and over again with sponsorship opportunities as a result.

The main thing is keeping content coming. Consistency is important. Over the years I've waxed and waned with consistency- starting out at publishing no less than four days per week, and after an illness and a third move, I was posting whenever I had the time and the strength. (Thankfully, at one point, I had a team of guest writers who kept regular and value-packed content flowing on my blog. I'll talk about guest posting later on in the book.)

The key is to remember that routine is important. Maybe you're a schedule person and like things posted on your calendar to help you remember exactly when to do things. At least that's how I operate. These days, I couldn't run a business (or my life in general) without Google Calendar.

Take some time to figure out how many blog posts you'd like to attempt each week, then put it on your calendar. Simple as that.

One thing I like to do nowadays is to plan my blog post topics for the entire year. I know it sounds overwhelming, but it really isn't and it simplifies the blogging process for me. This doesn't mean that I don't deviate from it at times, but having an idea of what topics I will blog about each month keeps me on track and keeps me sane. Today I don't post as often to my blogs as I did back in the beginning, but knowing in advance what my topics are helps me to plan more effectively.

My favorite tool for writing down my thoughts and planning out my ideas is Evernote. (I use Google docs too, but Evernote has been my go-to lately.) I simply begin a new note and list out the months. Each month gets its own section and I like to plan four possible topics per month (a minimum of one blog post per week.)

Again, as I mentioned before, life happens, and I don't always get around to blogging as regularly as I'd like. However, at the beginning of my blog launch, getting out regular posts was a definite priority for me as I paved my way toward getting noticed in Google. Try to define a specific amount of posts you'd like to write each week and begin writing!

SCHEDULING POSTS

I learned this trick earlier on. Scheduling out my posts gave me a head start for those days I didn't feel like writing a thing.

What you'll want to do is carve out some time (maybe 2 hours or so) where you'll do nothing but batch schedule. What is batch scheduling? It's a brilliant idea that I wish I had thought of sooner in my blogging career.

Basically, I sit down in front of my computer with a list of keywords and blog post ideas I've gathered. From this resource as well as my list of topics I've planned for the year, half-year, or month, I am now armed with the ammunition to knock those posts out of the way!

Batch scheduling to me is like blogging on steroids. Rather than waiting each week to figure out what to write about, I first develop outlines for those topics I've planned on blogging about.

And just to briefly mention again, you do need to enjoy writing if you plan to build a business blog. However, if you're not a prolific writer, no worries. In the blogging world, you can really and truly simplify. The outlines can be as simple as a topic (or thesis) statement for the introductory paragraph, point one and details, point two and details, point three and details, conclusion paragraph. I like to stick with 3-pointers because they're easy and short and they seem to get the point across. If your goal is to sell handcrafted necklaces, you really don't need to worry about blogging about your kids' school or what you had for dinner last week. Don't worry about what others typically blog about. You don't need a "mommy" blog in the typical sense in order to make money. You just need a blog to help you serve your customers and attract new ones. And if a mommy blog is what makes you money, then do your thing!

Next after my outline is writing the articles. This is where my 2-hour slot comes in handy. I'll take this to write as many articles as I can based on my outlines. Within two hours, I can at least write two or three posts at once (sometimes a bit more if I'm ambitious).

My advice is at first, shoot for one article per hour, and eventually, you'll find yourself churning one out in 30 minutes. Relax and let the love flow as you write about a topic you enjoy to an audience who will love you for it. It's amazing how the content will spill out of you if you give yourself the room to simply focus on doing the one task: creating content.

After my posts are written, I go ahead and schedule them out in WordPress. Another reason I love WordPress so much is the ability to automate tasks. There are also plenty of great plugins to look into for scheduling posts (a quick google search will turn up quite a few results). You could use a variety of free plugins or step it up a notch and use the Editorial Calendar plugin. When you're ready to schedule your posts on social media later on you can use Hootsuite, Buffer, and Postify to name a few. Get them scheduled out for the next two weeks. Then my advice is to repeat this process all over again in a few days.

You could even carve out an entire week if you want, of doing nothing but creating posts in advance. This way, you won't even have to think about it or feel bad for letting your blog slide for several months. (And I've done that.) Believe me, when I'm all caught up and even ahead of the game, it serves me well for those days and weeks when I just can't get around to blogging. So batch scheduling is definitely worth it.

What if you don't want to "batch schedule"?

Never mind, you don't have to! Really, it's no big deal. Just blog when you can. Try to set aside a few hours each week to write up and edit a post. (Keep in mind that writing just one post includes a few miniature tasks which I'll talk about soon, so give yourself the time and space for creating good, quality content.)

If you do better writing when the kids are in bed, then by all means- set up shop after dark. If you're a morning person, wake up at the crack of dawn, grab your cup of coffee and computer and start blogging! Whatever floats your boat.

Personally, I prefer mid-afternoon blogging (right after lunch and after we homeschool) to get my personal work done while the kids busy themselves with their own hobbies. I'm also a morning person, but mornings rarely work for us anymore since I've committed that time for schooling my kids. Sometimes when we're out and about for music or dance lessons, I grab that time to get a bit of work done at a nearby coffee shop or even in the waiting room with other parents.

The point is, you can find the time to blog even if you choose not to do it all at once. Feel free to blog whenever you can and however you can.

Batch scheduling is simply one option that, in my opinion, simplifies the blogging process. I like it because when I'm already in writing mode, I can get a lot of posts done at once without breaking my stride (unless a kid needs school work help or needs a snack, that is.)

Do it the way that works best for you- but do begin scheduling your blog posts.

CREATING THE PERFECT BLOG POST

When you create a blog post you want it to be significant enough to have an impact on your readers without giving it all away. (Meaning, if you're a life coach, don't tell all your coaching strategies in your first week of blogging. Give your readers time to get to know you and drop subtle hints, leading them to your business.)

You also want to make sure you have all the basics in place. So I thought I'd share with you a briefing on the anatomy of a blog post.

THE ANATOMY OF A BLOG POST

First, you have your **blog title**, which should be catchy enough to peak your readers' interest. It should definitely include your keywords for that post. For example, if you want to teach your readers how to make homemade, organic dog biscuits, those exact words should be in your title:

How To Make Organic Homemade Dog Biscuits

Secondly, the body of your post consists of the content you're sharing. That content should be long enough to deliver value (no one-paragraph posts for the most part) and should include your chosen keywords throughout the body of the post as well in your meta tags.

If you're not familiar with meta tags, just think of them as little keywords within your blog post that Google sees to give it an idea of what your post is about. WordPress gives you a place to add your keywords, and if you're using a plugin like Yoast SEO, you'll have an opportunity to plug in your keywords again. For the optimal SEO experience, try to fit your main keyword in your title and a few times throughout the body of the post.

The most important piece of this would be your title tags and meta description. For each post make sure you fill out the meta description to include a brief summary of what the post is about (including the keywords).

Meta-what?

A meta title gives Google information about your blog post. Make sure it's relevant by including the keywords pertaining to your topic. It is by default the post title but is editable. Google sees the title as very important, so optimize this before you worry about other meta tags. Keep it short and simple (Google only reads around the first 70 characters.) It needs to grab attention quickly, as it will be what encourages your visitors to click.

Meta descriptions tell what your post is about. Make sure, again, to use your relevant keywords. Google is looking for relevancy based on what your readers were searching for. Your post will become more relevant to Google as it sees your blog as the solution to what your visitors are searching for.

The following example shows the key phrase "making money from home" showing up in my blog post title (in blue) and again in my description underneath (in bold).

👁 Snippet preview

019:Making money from home:Ideas for work at home moms - Mompren...
www.mompreneursinheels.com/blog/work-at-home-moms-making-money-home-ideas/
Work at home moms can be **making money from home**. With this list of ideas you may find an opportunity that works for you.

✏ Edit snippet

making money from home

And again, a title tag and meta description as show in Google results.

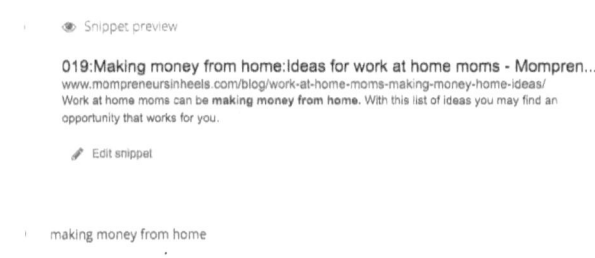

Again, you can easily do all of this with a plugin such as Yoast SEO. From your end of things, all you need to do is write up the post, give it a fabulous title and clear description, and remember to throw in those keywords!

Your next blog post layer is media. For **images,** you'll want to make them big enough to be easily viewable on your post. In order to be Pinterest-ready, it's always a great idea to have your images watermarked with your blog post URL. Also, it doesn't hurt to download the Pinterest Pin-It plugin to give your readers the opportunity to pin your post. In general, most blog post images look generally good on screen at around pixels 500x400 pixels or greater. I generally use the dimensions 750x400 on one of my blogs. This would, of course, all depend on your template layouts, but this is what works for me.

Videos and audio are other forms of media I tend to use a lot on my blogs. If you plan to take this extra step in your posts, starting with video is generally easiest in my opinion, simply because you can access quick embed forms from either Vimeo or YouTube right onto your blog- whereas podcasting takes just a few extra steps to get going. However, I do recommend podcasting, but only after you've considered the work involved in blogging, have a handle on it, and don't mind the extra work it takes to run a podcast. While I think podcasting is an excellent way to promote your brand and get your name out there I also feel the duty of being honest about the labor surrounding the process of it.

Use video, use audio, use images, use keywords, use a great title- and most of all, use your passions! The truest core of the blog post is your passion and drive: your voice.

Now let's dig into more details of what a blog post should entail.

Be relatable

When you create a blog post, you'll want to always remember that your content should connect you with your reader on a personal level.

Relate to your reader and make the post personal and talk about your own experiences. Engage them.

Make it easy to read and understand

For those of us who tend to be wordy (*raising my hand here*), it can be difficult to be concise and right to the point. Your reader is looking for a solution to a problem, for entertainment, or a tutorial on how to do something specific. Be concise, stay on topic, and choose your words carefully. Make it very clear what your post is about and follow through from beginning to end.

Be visually appealing

This goes back to the DIY graphic design we talked about earlier. As a blogger, my suggestion regarding making your own graphics is a definite yes. If you can afford a VA (virtual assistant), by all means, hire it out. Otherwise, go ahead and count on creating post graphics as being a part of your daily (or weekly) blogging routine.

For each blog post, you'll want to include a blog image. (If you're relaunching and you don't have images, go back through all of your posts and begin creating images for them. Yes, I know it's a lot of work, but you will be glad you did, and proud of yourself. Tell me about it, and I'll be proud of you, too!)

Which means, if you're not already, you'll need to get comfortable with image editing programs. I use Photoshop quite a bit, but I've found some really user-friendly services online that are free, like PicMonkey and Canva. Grab free stock images by doing a google search for "free stock images". If you want to invest part of your budget in stock images, places like iStockPhoto have decent, quality photos. If you don't like their prices, sticking with free images can work out quite well. Also, if you own a really nice camera, use it! My Canon Rebel has allowed me to take beautiful background shots that I could use for a blog post image. You want big, bold, beautiful photos to not only accompany your post but to draw in your readers from platforms like Pinterest.

Be yourself and enjoy the process because next, we'll talk about how your passion can help you create long-lasting connections.

CHAPTER 8: MAKE FABULOUS, LIKE-MINDED CONNECTIONS.

Making connections online is a great way to grow your business. This chapter will take you into the importance of getting out there online and working your marketing magic. And while you might not feel you have that part together, just know that it's easier than it sounds.

First things first. While I don't plan to get into the specifics of social media in this book (there are plenty other books and resources that can help you determine which platform is best for you), I do want to point out how imperative it is that you do choose a few and get involved. Grab your brand name (or your actual name) for places like Twitter and Facebook and establish a presence there. For example, when I first started my blog, ChristianHomeschoolMoms.com, I immediately set out to grab a Twitter handle and start a Facebook page. I also opened up accounts with Pinterest, YouTube, Google Plus, and LinkedIn. My goal was to establish my presence on social media even if I didn't plan to use each of those platforms to the fullest. That's the first part.

Once you've covered your basics and have accounts, you'll now want to focus on the few social media platforms where you are pretty certain your target audience hangs out. Since I'm reaching moms in business, Twitter, Facebook and Pinterest are great choices for me. Also, since I run a podcast, I chose to submit my show to iTunes, since I know a lot of moms love listening to the kind of information I share while they run errands. Find your favorite social media spots and start to camp out there. See what works for you, where you get the most engagement. Currently, I'm trying my hands at Periscope and getting a feel for it. So far, it's not my favorite (I'm a YouTube gal.) But I like the concept and I'm attempting to make it work for a bit to see if it's useful for my business at all. If over a certain period of time I find a lack of interest and engagement, I won't continue to put my efforts there. If I like it, however, it becomes a part of my social media strategy. So, really, you just have to try and see what works and what doesn't. We entrepreneurs are all doing the same thing out here: trial and error.

WAYS TO CONNECT

Connection with social media

Looking beyond social media, let's talk about connecting with our audience. Remember the principles I discussed earlier about engagement? This is the stage in your business where reaching out and connecting with your prospects is vital.

When you create a blog post, then talk about it, you begin to spur conversation on social media. You'll want to tweet each post, pin to Pinterest, share on Facebook or hop over to YouTube, Google Hangouts, Facebook Live, Periscope, or even a podcast to talk about it. Notice, **you** have to talk it about it first! Nobody is going to do this part of the job for you.

Although a naturally chatty person, I tend to veer on the introverted side at times. This means it can be hard for me to promote myself. However, when I'm quiet on social media, when I don't promote my products or services, **nobody knows about them!** If you don't speak up, nobody will. You'll have to get out there and make some noise.

Joining online groups

While it's important we become our own spokesperson and talk about our products and services with confidence, we should also keep in mind that connecting online is not all about promoting ourselves. It's also about reaching out to form relationships with other like-minded individuals.

You can do this through joining online groups via Facebook or Google Plus and other social media networks you like best. I find my biggest community of connection to be through my podcasts and YouTube channels. My podcast spurs direct responses to me- for suggestions on new show topics to an occasional thanks which always makes my day. My YouTube channel feels like a mini support group and is a way for me to share my ideas and receive feedback, as well as give my viewers an opportunity to support one another in the comments.

When I subscribe to someone's channel or follow someone on social media, I'm looking for a place to contribute as well as to receive support.

Having a two-way mindset regarding giving + receiving is important in what is often referred to as "relationship marketing". You don't just go out there in the blogosphere and social media to blast your message and leave. You go on the lookout for connections. You want to make friends. You want to find people to support. You also want to find those a few steps (or many steps) ahead of you to support you. You go ready to serve, and allow yourself the grace to be served.

When you meet a potential client online, befriend them. Take time with them personally, encourage them, promote them, and let that person know about your services and how you may be of help to them when the time comes (which is usually not right off the bat.)

Don't be *that* mompreneur that joins multiple Facebook groups in order to blast promotionals about her business. Not only is it a huge turn-off, but most moderators will kick you out of the group quickly. (I'm speaking from experience since I once moderated a Google Plus group for business women and found that 98% of the members used the group to promote their business with no intention of ever contributing value to the group.) I believe I'm talking to the choir, here, and I'm certain that if you've gotten this far in the book, you have every intention of bringing your best to the table wherever you go.

Let's flip things for a moment and talk about the benefits of reaching out to others online. When you begin contributing to your groups, you begin meeting people virtually. These people are either in your niche market or they have the potential to become your own customer or client. Either way, you can leverage these two instances and make the best of your connections.

If I feel that a certain group has my prospects, I become intentional about finding out how to make an introduction so that I can share what I do with the group. I have found clients this way. If questions are asked that I feel I have the expertise to answer, then by being quick to respond and give credible answers I have set myself up as an expert within the group.

For this type of interaction, you have to join the right groups and become very familiar with the nature of them and how to post. Know the rules, the moderators' likes and dislikes, and do your best to help the moderator by providing value to the group. In this way, you can establish a good reputation for your business and make valuable connections.

Mastermind groups

On other groups, you might find yourself the novice. This is where you have the opportunity to ask for advice and coaching. Many mompreneurs join mastermind groups which are quite helpful in supporting your own business growth. Through your personal business needs and questions, you can find invaluable advice and quality connections with experts right at your fingertips.

Interviews

I also find that these types of groups give me leads for my podcast. When I find an expert in her field, I contact her and ask for an interview at my podcast, which leads to an even deeper connection because now we're speaking on a more personal level- on the phone.

What I've found about networking is this: when you find exceptional business models, take the time to learn from the masters. If I notice a YouTuber who is just plain awesome, I'll schedule in some time to reach out to connect with her and see if we can connect on a deeper level. This usually begins with a series of emails and an invitation to be a guest on my podcast. Through these connections, I've been able to learn from the best, as well as grow my own business. Anytime I make a connection with an Influencer, she introduces me to her tribe as well, and my circle of influence becomes wider and deeper. This is the value of reaching out and connecting.

Guest posting

What is your expertise? For an extra boost in your blog visibility, consider guest posting at blogs within your niche. For several years I contributed as a regular contributor to several well-known homeschooling blogs. I committed to a once-monthly schedule for 3 different blogs (while keeping up with my own three blogs at the time!), and though I was overscheduled (I don't recommend that pace), I benefited greatly from those contributions.

Each time I submitted a post, my author bio was attached to the end of the post. The author bio is that short snippet of information about who you are plus your headshot photo and blog URL. It is oh-so-beneficial in driving quality traffic back to your site because it places your face and name on the radar of that blog's readers and introduces you to a whole new crowd who had never heard of your blog before.

Provided you've added that email subscription box on your site (the one we talked about earlier), then as the reader sees your URL on the guest post that **you've** written and clicks on your link, she will likely join your mailing list. That's why it's important to plan out your blog efficiently at the very beginning stage of business building.

For three years, I also invited guest posters on my own blog. Eventually it turned into the management of a small team of ten guest writers at my Christian Homeschool Moms blog. These writers were also homeschool moms who had much value to contribute to my blog through their own experiences as homeschoolers, and each month they all provided one post for my blog. This was helpful to me, as you can imagine, because it kept that much-needed content coming for my readers (and for Google!), and gave me a writing break. By the same token, my writers benefited from a backlink to their URL permanently placed on my blog as well as promotion opportunities on my podcast, and occasionally on my YouTube videos.

The beauty of the backlink is essentially having your blog URL associated with one of more prominence in Google ranking than yours. Google will often associate you with those blogs and you may get a small boost or lift in ranking as a result. So the saying "birds of a feather flock together" applies in relationship marketing. The lesson here is: reach out and make those online connections!

Media Kits

Another thing I want to briefly mention in this chapter is media kits. Media kits are public relation tools which help your company with exposure to your product or service. To explain it a bit further, I borrowed the following from investopedia.com:

"A media kit can be as simple as a page on a company's website or as complex as a package of information and product samples sent to selected members of the media that the company hopes will promote them. The media kit commonly provides the company's official name; the names, titles and biographies of its most important people; information about the company's history and function; photos; and any press releases the company has had written about itself. The media kit will also provide contact information for reporters who seek additional information or want to interview someone at the company."

Simplified, in your media kit you'll include your long bio and picture, the purpose of your blog, and your blog stats.

For an effective media kit, you'll need to know how to find and read your blog stats. Long, long ago I used Awstats (found in the dashboard of most hosting control panels), but today I can't recommend it. Google Analytics is the way to go.

Once you open your Analytics account, play around with it a bit and research how to read it so you're aware of what the numbers mean. Basically, you want to be sure to differentiate between "hits" and "unique visitors" which are totally different. Never go with the super-inflated "hits" number, which, according to OpenTracker.net, includes every single time a file has been sent to a browser by a web server. This means one person can reload your page 300 times and be counted as 300 hits to your site. Rather, you want to look closely at unique visitors- the number of visitors total who came to your blog. Even if they visited your blog 300 times in one month, they will only be counted as one visitor, not 300. This is a more reliable number for your blog stats to offer in your media kit.

Once you feel as though you have enough traction online, I recommend you go ahead and create a media kit. I created my first media kit at around only 2,000 unique visitors per month- and I recommend that at 1,000 (unique) visitors, you can go ahead and begin. So long as you have a specialty niche and a responsive list of subscribers, you can be selling ad space while simultaneously building your blog.

You'll want to do a bit of research before you set your pricing. Figure out what you want to sell: ad space, promos on your YouTube, or paid reviews, for example.

Determine what others in your market are selling ad space for. Ask around for advice. Join forums and groups to help you determine your market value.

Don't wait around too long. Setting up your blog as a business requires thinking about these things in advance. A media kit can get you on the road to multiple business connections. If you have a media kit on hand, you'll be prepared should a company request it and the opportunity arises for you to work with a brand.

Other revenue streams

Since we're on the topic of media kits, let's go ahead and

lay out some of your options for monetizing your blog (in addition to your regular source of income). I don't claim to be an expert in all of these, but you should definitely know about them and dig further into research.

One of my most familiar ways of blog monetization is creating my own **digital products**. This, by far, has been one of my most successful monetization tactics. I create a product (ebooks, digital courses, workshops), I set the price, and I sell it to my prospects. You can speak, consult, write (for magazines, other blogs, your own books even), and create digital products. Digital products may include audio, video, text, or pictures. Anything from a simple report or ebook to a full-out membership course comprised of video modules can you bring you the money.

You can also tack on digital products to your service based business. For example, if you provide web design services, adding a digital training product for DIYers on how to design their own sites would be a great add-on to your business. Simply choose the type of course you want to create: write an ebook, host a workshop or seminar, or pre-record tutorials or lectures. Package it up pretty. If you're not a designer, hire Fiverr to create covers for ebooks and digital products. Then you'll provide a download page complete with the materials to be watched, listened to, read, and downloaded by your buyer. For a quick setup, throw a Paypal button on and password protect the page. There are plenty of membership site apps to help you accomplish this. If you're selling an ebook, take advantage of Amazon which has it all set up for you.

Another way I monetize my site is through **services.** My original business model has been service-based, providing coaching and consulting to women entrepreneurs. I designed banners and blogs, gave SEO strategy sessions, and provided podcast consulting. Along with these services, I also created digital products. At the time of this writing, I am expanding my business to include more digital products as I scale back on one-to-one coaching.

If you're a product-based business, you can mix and match as well. Remember the earlier example of the organic pet boutique? They sold items for pets, but they also provided consulting during certain hours of the day. Say for instance you sell natural handmade soaps and body creams. You can also add on a service for those interested in learning more about healthy skin care: perhaps a free coaching call leading to a series of paid calls. Perhaps you give a paid workshop or speak at a natural health care event on natural skin products.

You can create your own services based on your products, and products based on your services. It's your business, and the sky's the limit! Mix and match how you like.

Many bloggers also use **ad revenue services** such as Google Adsense. Other services like this include Media.net, Bing, and Chitika. There are, of course, many more. There are networks you can join, such as [BlogHer](#) (and a host of others) that will give you opportunities to work with sponsors. For my homeschooling blog, I joined the iHomeschool Network which connects education companies with homeschool bloggers, providing bloggers an extra source of income when sponsorship and guest posting opportunities become available. My main source of income on my homeschooling blog has been selling ads and product reviews directly to homeschooling companies. Anytime I am asked to review a product, I send my media kit and if all goes well, I land a contract. With my coaching business at [DemetriaCreative.com](#), the bulk of my income is direct services (blog designs, podcast consulting, blog coaching and helps). As I make the shift into creating more digital products over at Mompreneurs In Heels, that is where I anticipate more of my income will accrue over the next few years.

Keep connections going.

So, you've made a few connections, and over time you don't keep in touch. This only means you lose your connections! My recommendation is to keep some type of interaction going. An occasional "hi, how are you?" through Facebook will suffice. You won't have time to say hello to everyone, but if you anticipate working with someone in particular in the future, it pays to keep the lines of communication open between you.

Be open and authentic.

I'm a private person at heart, but running a business online means that I need to be open to authenticity. I can't stay hidden behind my four walls, nor behind the screen. Eventually, I need to get out and network- both online and offline.

Being authentic means being willing to talk about your mistakes and mishaps. You don't dwell on them or talk down on yourself (no one is attracted to that), but you use your mistakes as an object lesson to help others.

There is a popular hair stylist whose mailing list is extremely responsive (they must be- she's a millionaire), and her emails are always filled with the latest and personal updates of her life. She includes an object lesson based on what she's going through personally. She helps her readers to connect with her in a personal way. When her mother-in-law passed away, we (her subscribers) knew about it. She told us her fears, her griefs, and her successes. This helps us to connect to her personally and feel more inclined to buy her products because we feel as though we know her.

Don't forget to be real. It will make a **huge** difference.

Also, get out in your community and begin making connections. If you hear of a blogging conference near you, hop on board. I like to attend business training programs and mixers. We have free ones in our community at the local libraries, and you can oftentimes find seminars and meet and greets through your library or community center. Check with your community and see what's available, and join in the fun!

Chapter 9: Find your stride and work it!

As I would say to my closest friends, "You're on the roll, girlfriend!"

Here you are- blogging and promoting your business. Now your main job is to keep the flow going. Keep your stride. If you don't yet have your stride, create your blogging calendar and stick with it, figure out your routine, and hit play and repeat each week.

Finding your groove is paramount to your success after creating your blog and making connections. You have to keep the momentum going or you lose ground. If that means batch scheduling your blog posts, or taking short breaks but coming back with a vengeance, figure out a system that's workable for you and your family. Speaking of which, we'll get into family life in just a moment.

Finding and maintaining your routine

The first thing you should do is make a list of all of your weekly, monthly, and annual blogging goals. From there you go into reverse engineering and figure out what you need to do *each* month, *this* month, and *this week* in order to meet your blogging goals for the year. Your annual goals can look anything like this:

- Increase mailing list by 50% by the end of the year
- Reach goal of 500/1,000/5,000 followers on Facebook by the end of December
- Grow Twitter following by 300 by the end of

November.
- Produce $2,000/$5,000/$10,000 in sales by the end of the first year.
- Add 5 new products to my product line by mid-October.

And your goals don't always have to be hard and fast numbers. Those initial annual goals can sometimes be the hardest to make because you are projecting something that hasn't yet happened. However, I do want to caution you not to be too hard on yourself here. Do be reasonable. If you are just starting out with 0 mailing list subscribers and your website is brand new, don't set a goal for 500 new subs per month. Maybe consider ten new subs the first month a success, then 20-50 the second month, and so forth. Give yourself flexibility when thinking through the process and understand that in reverse engineering there is work involved to achieve these goals. Consider how much time and energy you have to invest in what it takes to reach your goals, and also consider family life. Do you have sicknesses and doctor's visits? Does your spouse have a new job? Are your kids enrolled in a new school this year? Life transitions are a reality and will influence the time you have to commit to your business goals, so plan accordingly.

If you feel confident that your business goals are accurate for your lifestyle and what you are willing to handle, now it's time to reverse engineer your goals.

BEGIN WITH THE END IN MIND. A SIMPLE EXAMPLE OF REVERSE ENGINEERING

Let's say for instance your goal is to grow your list by 150% by the end of the year. You have 12 months. You have 200 people on your list currently and you need to change this number over time in order to have a substantial customer base. Now let's think about the steps you would take in order to help you achieve this goal.

Initial Tasks:

Make sure that the email subscription box is located visibly on each page of the blog.

Make sure to include social media share icons on each page of the blog. (Use a social sharing plugin such as Shareaholic, for example.)

Make good use of tools such as delayed subscription box pop-ups. (Some people call them annoying, but they really do help to grow your list if you do it just right.)

Create a CTA (call to action) on Facebook page, YouTube channel, and all social media.

Monthly Tasks:

- Write 12-20 blog posts. This increases targeted traffic with regular and ongoing keyword-rich content.
- Create a post as a guest blogger once per month, and invite them to join your mailing list with a CTA.
- Produce two videos or podcasts and encourage signups.
- Comment on others' blog posts. Goal: 20 comments. This helps to increase your visibility on the web.
- Set up a tweet in Hootesuite for each new blog post (at least 8 per month per blog post.)
- Share all new blog posts on Google Plus, Facebook fan page and groups, and Pinterest.
- Participate in focus groups or create online events (Facebook Live, for example)-about 8 per month. Always use these events to invite viewers to sign up for your mailing list.
- Create a new freebie, giveaway, or contest to

obtain new subscribers once each quarter-every three months.

Weekly Tasks:

- Write 3-5 new blog posts.
- Comment on others' blogs 5 times per week.
- Tweet each new blog post at least twice per week.
- Share each new blog post on Google Plus, Facebook fan page and groups, and Pinterest.
- Participate in focus groups or create online events (YouTube, Facebook Live)-about twice per week.

Today's Tasks:

- Write a blog post.
- Add a tweet and Facebook share of the post to the Hootesuite scheduler.
- Pin post on Pinterest.
- Share post on Google Plus.
- Lead Facebook Live webinar.
- Respond to all social media comments.
- Read and comment on at least one blog post of someone in my niche or target market.
- Write an outline for tomorrow's YouTube video.

I hope this sample schedule gives you an idea of how you can begin to cycle through your process of sustaining your online business for the long haul. It just takes a long term goal- in this case, one year-to create a master plan. With that plan, you can break down your monthly, weekly, then daily blogging plan goals. This reverse engineering method works very well for me.

However, I do have my seasons when life isn't so pretty and neatly packaged and doesn't quite fit into my blogging plan. During those seasons it's still 100% better to have had a plan to begin with and to be able to get back on track than to never have had a plan at all.

Avoiding burnout

When those seasons of burnout happen- and they definitely can- you should have a plan of action in place.

I hesitate to write this part of the chapter because I'm just so stoked that you are on this blogging journey! The last thing I want to do is dissuade a mompreneur from continuing along the path of the multiple streams of income that can happen through blogging. But I need to be honest. Burnout can happen, and it can happen fast. That is unless you take the necessary precautions against blogging burnout.

In order to avoid burnout, I recommend not adding too much on your plate at once. By this I mean, be careful of balancing multiple blogs. At this time, I run two active blogs. There were times I was balanced four blogs at once. Running this many blogs requires a lot of time and effort to give each one proper attention. Of course, many of my blogs went lacking in updates for months and spreading myself out that thin meant that I couldn't properly devote the time necessary for each of them. Although I was able to accrue some income from each of them, I could have better monetized one blog than four blogs at once. By focusing my energy on just one or two blogs, I could better devote myself to leveraging just those two blogs for more income.

Also, avoid overcommitting to your clientele and customers. If you plan to publish a workshop by the end of next month, don't promise it by two weeks' time. If you know you'll need two hours to update your blog and you can only handle one design client that week, don't commit to three clients. Updating your blog is an integral part of your business- helping to grow and maintain additional clients. Maybe you could commit to one client now and open up available time slots again in three weeks. If they are truly committed to receiving your help, your clients would much rather wait on you than to have you burning the candles at both ends to satisfy them and other clients simultaneously-if you can't handle it all. To your tribe and followers, your word means more than its weight in gold. They trust you, so keeping your word and keeping their trust is important. So, no over-commitments. And keep your blogging commitments consistent.

Another thing to consider is changing your blogging commitments. If you mainly receive customers by word of mouth, or you manage to sell your products through Etsy or on consignment, you may find that having a blog seems more secondary to you. Although I don't encourage you to walk away from blogging, I would advise you to consider how often you blog and whether or not a daily blogging schedule is beneficial to your business model. It's okay to scale back, so long as you keep blogging a built-in part of your system. Shoot for at least once per week if you need to, but try to keep content flowing on a regular basis. You never want to give up on your blogging presence altogether.

Remember earlier we talked about the different ways to monetize your blog? Even if you mostly sell products offline, you can never underestimate the power of your blog bringing a huge potential fan base to your brand. You want to stay aware and relevant online as well as offline. Selling those handmade soaps may be one way you're making money at a farmer's market today, but may lead to a digital product further down the road, teaching others how to create their own handmade soaps. It might be that later down the road you attract brands or partners who want to work with you. Your blog has great potential.

So, keep your balance and scale back if you need to. There is no requirement in the blogging world that says you have to blog five days a week. I don't blog that often, and there are, admittedly, times when I don't blog for two weeks straight due to life circumstances. Not recommended, but life happens. (Which is why batch scheduling can save the day).

This leads me to the next topic: the ultimate mompreneur balance. How do mompreneurs do it all?

BALANCING FAMILY LIFE WITH BUSINESS

So, here's the critical part of the life of a mompreneur: balancing family life with business. If your household is anything like mine, your kids and spouse have busy schedules throughout the school year, which means you have a lot of time management issues to deal with. The house also needs to be cleaned, dinner cooked, quality time spent with the kids (and hubs), and there needs to be time left in the day for you to take a breather. You need time to just be you: exercise, listen to music, read a book, paint your nails, start a DIY project from an idea you found on Pinterest. The key is balance.

Life balance is crucial to your success as a mom in business. Without it, nothing works. The reason I talk about having blogging systems in place, making plans and creating routines is because you'll be more able to find the balance you need with family when you know exactly what you need for your business.

The most important factor for me, however, is not having my business plans lined up in a neat row as much as it is making sure my family is taking care of. First and foremost, the systems I create for my family life have to be taken care of and supersede anything I do to contribute financially. Because my husband also works full time, is in the U.S. Navy Reserve, and is the main breadwinner for our family, it helps if one of us keeps family life running on the home front. Because I've chosen to be home, the priority of keeping our home life running smoothly has fallen into my lap. Therefore, anything I choose to do financially for the family is currently an addition to our finances. This means that in my personal family life, the way I choose to order my lifestyle places family and home life first and business after.

That said, with blogging routines that work like clockwork, I know exactly how my family routines and household duties usually fall around that. For me, my personal routine looks like this:

6-8 a.m.- business blogging, recording a video, or podcasting

8-12 p.m.- homeschooling

12-1- lunch break

1-4ish— office time: business blogging, social media, and more

4:30-start dinner

5-8- family time/evening family activities/workout

8-10- kids' bedtime routines/more family time

10-11-night time blogging wrap-ups

11-bed

Some afternoons I don't have office time and can't blog because I'm out running errands or taking the kids to an activity. On those days I might extend my night work a bit to compensate, or I may choose to get up earlier the next morning. The best way to establish business routines whether you're spending more of your time at home, or working around your 9-5, is to get a routine going that works around your day job (or home life).

If you're a working mom, you might try fitting some blogging into your lunch break, and perhaps one hour in the morning before work and an hour or two after work before you come home. Use the time you have allotted with care, zeroing in on the specific blogging tasks you have in front of you without getting distracted. If your coworkers are all heading out to a restaurant every day for lunch, you may want to decline a few times a week and take a hiatus to your nearest coffee shop to get some work done.

If you're working from home like me, you may first try to establish some regular home routines for your kids and for housework. Think about what you'd like your regular work hours to be and begin leaving those time slots free for blogging. If you have younger kids, establishing nap times, snack times, and the help you need to get through your day's work. And by the way, it never hurts to ask a friend or relative for help or hire a mother's helper once a week. With younger children at tow, dwindling down those work hours to 30 minutes or 1 hour at a time may be all you can do for now. Believe me, I get it! For years, I snatched what few precious hours of work I could during my toddler's nap times.

As my children grew older, I learned to work around their school schedule (after our homeschool mornings) and in between lunch and dinner times. Now with one teen in the house plus a big kid, I have to somehow fit blogging into busy school days filled with music and art lessons, dance lessons, learning groups, church activities, and field trips.

Although I'm busier with the kids now, it's much easier to actually get work done since they are older and understand that mom works a few hours per day.

My advice: while your kids are young, do what you can with the time you have available to you and be faithful to it. In due time, you'll have more availability to your work as your kids grow older, and it won't be so difficult. Also, as your kids grow older, teach them to appreciate the work you do. Allow them to help you with some of your work tasks from time to time, and reward them for helping you. Every time you tuck away at your desk to blog and your kids need to keep busy, reward them when they've done well. Spend extra time with them when you're done and let them know how proud you are of them for helping mom to get work done for her business!

Become a lifelong learner

I have never stopped learning, and I never will. It doesn't matter how much I think I know about a topic, there is just always more to learn. No matter how many training programs I develop, I will always take the time to learn from someone who knows a lot more than I do.

A big piece of advice I have for mompreneurs is to become lifelong learners. Find skills you're lacking in and find someone who has those skills- then set out to learn more about that topic. The more knowledge and understanding you attain, the greater the potential for your business to expand.

This goes back to my topic on joining mastermind groups or focus groups. If you align yourself with others who are pursuing what you are pursuing or who have more wisdom than you and are willing to share that wisdom with you, then you should open your arms to embrace all that life is offering you. This is your opportunity to position yourself to learn from the masters. (I personally consider anyone who knows more than I do on a topic a master at his or her trade.)

How do I become a lifelong learner? I join focus groups on Facebook or Google Plus. I listen to business mentoring podcasts and subscribe to YouTube channels. I purchase training programs from thought leaders whom I admire and follow them on LinkedIn and Periscope. I also subscribe to technical training programs on places like lynda.com.

There are many ways to become a lifelong learner. Attend in-person or virtual conferences, watch webinar replays, purchase ebooks (and read library books), or hire a coach. Any and all of these ideas can work depending on your needs. The main thing is: never stop learning.

Chapter 10: Time to Celebrate!

Alright, lady, it's time to celebrate! You have come a long way. You should feel extremely proud of yourself. I am proud of us both. It took me exactly one year to pound out this book after several setbacks (illness, moving to a different city, and a stolen laptop, plus the fear that I'd lost all my content for this book before I realized it was in Dropbox after all.) When you've come this far, you absolutely, without a shadow of a doubt, must celebrate your successes!

Before we begin talking about how to celebrate, let's briefly have a word of caution here: **celebrating yourself is okay, but comparing yourself is not.**

So often women believe that everyone else, anyone else, deserves to be complimented, appreciated, and celebrated. But when it comes down to applauding ourselves, we may be tempted to brush it off, shrug our shoulders and say "Oh, it was no big deal", when in reality, it was a *huge* deal that you could pull something off so awesome. Take ownership of your successes.

On the other hand, another mistake many women make is comparing our successes with those of other women. I've seen it happening in the blogging world so often and it breaks my heart to see and hear the discouragement when a mompreneur should be proud of herself. It also hurts to hear the criticism of other moms. For example, I might hear the following from a blogging mom:

"I finally got my blog launched, but…it's nothing like hers. I doubt my blog could ever get that big."

"I want to write for XYZ blog. But I don't know. Who would care about my little blog? I barely have any reach online."

"How the heck does that mom have time to get anything done? I mean, really. She *must* be neglecting something. I could never accomplish that much. How is she doing it?"

"Okay, how did her Pinterest image get repinned over 80 times? My pins never get shared!"

"Forget Facebook! It's working for everyone else, just not for me."

"She's probably just buying her traffic."

"She's got 9 kids and she has time to grow her blog and attend conferences? Does she hire a nanny?"

These can be quite discouraging words and I hear them from mom bloggers on a regular basis. On this chapter about celebration, I have to bring attention to the negative words we often speak over ourselves and other mompreneurs so that we can think more deeply and clearly about the kind of energy we want to attract to ourselves. In order to truly celebrate, **we must first give honor where honor is due.** We must first give recognition to those who have achieved, and give a nod of approval to another mompreneur. Only when you've celebrated another woman's successes will your successes be celebrated more fully and completely. Jealous energy and positive energy just don't mix.

Now that I've gotten that word of warning out of the way, let's get back to the business of celebrating! As I mentioned before, sometimes as moms we are so accustomed to patting someone else on the back that we might not actually know how to celebrate ourselves. It took me a few years to warm up to the idea of giving myself a victory night, but here's how I did it:

During my first few years in business, the way I rewarded myself was with a weekly drink from Starbucks. Although I spent an exorbitant amount of time working at coffee shops, I refused to purchase a drink (tall mochas four times per week can really add up.) So, the permission I gave myself was the reward of my favorite drink at the end of each week for all the hard work I'd put in.

With time, I slowly learned to celebrate in other ways. I might give myself a day off for play by going to explore in the city or buy myself something I've been really wanting. Sometimes I'll meet up with friends I haven't seen in a while and have some girl time. My favorite celebration ritual is going out for dinner with my family. Seeing my husband and daughters seated around the table at Olive Garden or Red Lobster (our family faves), I remember what I've been working so hard to achieve.

Find whatever celebration ritual works for you, and be sure to do it! Whether it's a glass of your favorite sparkly drink, going on a shopping spree, or taking a bubble bath with relaxing music in an empty house, find out what brings you smiles and go for it! You deserve it!

Another way to celebrate is to reward your customers. I'm currently working on a system to keep my customers even happier by rewarding them with bonus perks for buying my products. This means more sales and coupon codes just for my regulars, more raffles and giveaways and chances to win both my products and my consulting, and once in a while, an exciting freebie just for being loyal.

Let's say you've reached 500 likes on Facebook. That's an especially awesome feeling and a great milestone to celebrate. You can reward yourself personally (go out for a night on the town with your girlfriends or have a date night with the hubs), as well as create a fun celebration such as a giveaway to reward your Facebook fans. Whatever you do, make it fun and make it something that you look forward to. The key in celebrating business life is creating milestones to look forward to and working methodically, dutifully, and faithfully until you reach your goals. When your goals are met, don't hesitate to pat yourself on the back and appreciate yourself. When you appreciate your successes, others will too.

The final wrap-up

Well, you have arrived. Congratulations are definitely in order. You are at the completion of this book, but beginning another leg (or a brand new one) of your adventurous, blogging journey. You have covered so much information to help you in beginning and continuing a solid online business.

I feel confident that with this valuable information I've given you on how to turn your passion, purpose, and vision into a profit, that you now have a blueprint for online business success. Let this not be just another book packed with information, but let it be a true foundation for your business.

My hopes for you are that you will blog your way to success. I wish you the very best in your endeavors to growing your business online. You can reach me for additional business support at mompreneursinheels.com. There, you can join my mailing list, listen in to the Mompreneurs In Heels Podcast. I'm here to help moms in business put your best foot forward online, and I'd love to connect with you and support you in your blogging endeavors.

If this book has been a blessing to your life and adds to

your business knowledge base, I would appreciate a review on Amazon!

And lastly, as I like to end my podcasts: **To Your Web Success!**

Demetria

Blog: MompreneursInHeels.com

Podcast: http://www.mompreneursinheels.com/podcast-2/

Twitter: https://twitter.com/websuccesscoach

Pinterest: http://www.pinterest.com/christianhsmoms

Instagram: https://www.instagram.com/mompreneursinheels/

YouTube: https://www.youtube.com/channel/UCyqQhMxp3uOuiXprWcx03cw

www.ingramcontent.com/pod-product-compliance
Lightning Source LLC
Chambersburg PA
CBHW031425210526
45464CB00005B/2056